D0522148

KATHERINE D. WATSON

Dr Crippen

———

the national archives

First published in 2007 by
The National Archives
Kew, Richmond
Surrey, TW9 4DU, UK
www.nationalarchives.gov.uk

The National Archives
brings together the Public Record Office,
Historical Manuscripts Commission,
Office of Public Sector Information
and Her Majesty's Stationery Office.

A catalogue card for this book is available from the British Library.

ISBN 978 1 905615 15 5

Cover illustrations: portraits of Dr Crippen (akg-images),
Belle Elmore/Cora Crippen (left; akg-images) and
Ethel le Neve (right; Hulton Archive/Getty Images)
Jacket design and page typesetting by Goldust Design
Page design and plate section typesetting by Ken Wilson | point 918
Picture research by Gwen Campbell
Printed in Germany by
Bercker Graphischer Betreib GmbH & Co

Contents

===

MURDER AND MUTILATION

Hawley Harvey Crippen, alias Peter Crippen, alias Franckel; and Ethel Clara Le Neve, alias Mrs Crippen, and Neave

Description of Crippen: age 50, height 5ft 3 or 4, complexion fresh, hair light brown, inclined sandy, scanty, bald on top, rather long scanty moustache, somewhat straggly, eyes grey, bridge of nose rather flat, false teeth, medium build, throws his feet outwards when walking. May be clean shaven or wearing a beard and gold rimmed spectacles, and may possibly assume a wig. Somewhat slovenly appearance, wears his hat rather at back of head. Very plausible and quiet spoken, remarkably cool and collected demeanour. Speaks French and probably German; carries firearms. An American citizen, and by profession a doctor.

Description of Le Neve: a shorthand writer and typist, age 27, height 5ft 5, complexion pale, hair light brown (may dye same), large grey or blue eyes, good teeth, nice looking, rather long straight nose (good shape), medium build, pleasant, lady-like appearance. Quiet, subdued manner, talks quietly, looks intently when in conversation.

Police 'Wanted' poster,
July 1910

An Unforgettable Crime

In 1910 16 murderers were hanged in Britain, but today the name of only one of them stirs a flicker of recognition. Dr Hawley Harvey Crippen was the henpecked husband, romantic lover and infamous killer who nonetheless inspired mild sympathy in all those who heard his story. He was the first internationally known fugitive from justice, and the first to be tracked down by wireless; his trial for the murder of his blowsy wife attracted more attention than any other for fifty years. To those who lived through it, 1910 would be remembered chiefly as the 'Crippen year', and his crime as the Camden Town Murder, or the North London Cellar Murder — so-called because the remains of the ill-fated Mrs Crippen were found buried in the cellar of the home they shared at 39 Hilldrop Crescent, Camden Town.

The case against Crippen rested on circumstantial evidence —circumstantial, but weighty and persuasive. Any weak or missing links were strengthened or supplied by Crippen himself during cross-examination. He entangled himself in a web of lies which seemed increasingly incredible, leaving his defence counsel with the unenviable task of convincing a jury that regardless of the damning evidence, such a kind-hearted and popular man could not have poisoned his wife, mutilated her body and disposed of it piecemeal. One of the many reasons why the case gripped the public's attention was this novel juxtaposition of Crippen's geniality and brutality.

Another was the fact that Crippen had a young mistress, the demure and lovely Ethel Le Neve, who appropriated some of his wife's jewels and furs and fled with Crippen by sea — attired in boy's clothing — only to be caught by a Scotland Yard detective alerted by wireless telegraphy. This new technology (radio's forerunner) was invented in 1895 by Guglielmo Marconi and widely commercialized after the turn of the century. Boarding a faster ship, Chief Inspector Walter Dew arrested the runaway couple off the coast of Quebec, technology and global publicity having proved that fugitives from justice had nowhere to hide.

The forensic evidence comprised the third key feature of the case: the filleted human body parts found in Crippen's cellar demanded all the ingenuity and skill that modern forensic medicine could muster, and the quartet of experts called in became media heroes. Dew, 'the man who caught Crippen', worked tirelessly to bring the 'ordinary little man' to justice — in part no doubt to assuage a certain irritation at having allowed Crippen to escape in the first place — and the case crowned his career. It also launched the career of England's greatest medical detective, the pathologist Bernard Spilsbury, and brought a mysterious poison called hyoscine to public prominence.

Crippen himself may have been ordinary, but his crime, flight, arrest, trial and love for Ethel Le Neve were not; the newspaper press seized on the case like few others before it. Modern communications were critical to the functioning of the burgeoning international media, which circulated daily information about the case to meet avid public interest in the story. Newspapers and magazines, many illustrated, vied for news and photographs, and the case was one of the first instances of cheque-book journalism: journalists eagerly sought a confession and both Crippen and Le Neve sold their stories to the press.

And here, of course, is the final piece in the puzzle, the last of the many reasons for the longevity of the Crippen case: only two people, perhaps three, ever knew what really happened at Hilldrop Crescent in the early hours of 1 February 1910, and they took the secret to their graves. We think we know how and why this domestic tragedy of operatic proportions occurred, but much remains supposition and the mystery endures, made all the more intriguing by the elements of illicit sex and gruesome violence. A variety of new books on the case bear witness to a continuing fascination with the story of the little doctor, his actress wife and typist lover, and prove that we can still ask the questions asked by the public in 1910: what happened to Mrs Crippen? Whose remains were found in her cellar? If they were hers, who mutilated her body and buried it there? Who had the opportunity, the skill and the access? How did she die? If she was poisoned, where did this occur, and who administered the fatal dose?

The case papers held at the National Archives focus on the central figure in the story — the American with a dodgy medical degree who carried on business in England in a quasi-medical capacity and who was to pay a heavy price for an unhappy marriage. They also give us glimpses of the other principal characters: Cora Crippen, the wife who used the stage name Belle Elmore more from hope than necessity, and the girl who loved Crippen, his typist Ethel Le Neve. Much of what we know about the lives and loves of these enigmatic Edwardians comes from the statements they and their friends made to the highly compassionate Chief Inspector Dew.

HAWLEY HARVEY CRIPPEN

Crippen was born in Coldwater, Michigan, in July 1862. He was the only surviving child of dry goods merchant Myron Augustus Crippen and his wife Andresse. According to Erik Larson in *Thunderstruck*, young Crippen enjoyed a childhood of privilege: the family business was one of the most successful in a wealthy town. Under the influence of his grandfather, Philo Crippen (the family patriarch), he was raised as a Methodist, although he later converted to Roman Catholicism.

Myron and Andresse Crippen decided to leave Coldwater sometime during the 1870s, travelling west to California as so many other Americans had. Perhaps they went via Indiana: in his statement to Dew, Crippen said that he was educated in Coldwater, Indiana and California, before enrolling at the University of Michigan's school of homeopathic medicine in 1882. Homeopathy was, as it remains, an extremely popular alternative to traditional medicine. Founded in the early nineteenth century by the German physician Samuel Hahnemann, its guiding doctrines were that 'like cures like' and that the smaller the dose the more effective a medicine would be. This found favour with both doctors and patients, particularly those who were wary of the toxicity of drugs. In the United States, homeopathy was quickly integrated into the nineteenth-century medical marketplace. At least eleven homeopathic medical schools were set up, vying for students who wanted to gain a practical education that did not require many years of study.

Despite the fact that homeopathy acquired a significant following in Britain—at the creation of the National Health Service in 1948, homeopathic hospitals were the only non-regular establishments recognized—a traditional medical education in Victorian England was very different to that offered in Michigan. Aware of this, Crippen decided to enlarge his experience by travelling to London in 1883; as he put it, he 'attended various hospitals to see the operations'. Months later, testifying in his own defence against the charge of killing and cutting up his wife, he had to insist that he had 'never gone through a practical course of surgery' (he had studied it in theory only), and had never performed a post-mortem examination in his life (all trial quotes are from DPP 1/13 or Filson Young's *The Trial of Hawley Harvey Crippen*).

One of the hospitals that Crippen worked at during this first visit to London was the Royal Bethlem, which from its medieval origins had focused on caring for the insane (there were no cures for madness). Popularly known as Bedlam, it was the source of our word 'bedlam', which evokes scenes of wild uproar and confusion. Once a place where the fashionable went to gawp at the unfortunate lunatics within, by the late nineteenth century the asylum had begun to foster the development of the emerging medical speciality of psychiatry. Although still largely unable to offer a true therapy, Victorian medicine could at least alleviate some of the worst symptoms of insanity, by using sedatives to prevent patients from harming themselves or others. Crippen claimed that it was at the Bethlem that he first heard of hyoscine being used for this purpose, but that it was used to a large extent in American insane asylums.

Crippen remained in London for several months before returning to America later in 1883, where he entered the Homeopathic Hospital College in Cleveland, Ohio. Apart from 'theoretical surgery', we do not know what he studied there, but Larson reports that in March 1884 the *Coldwater Courier* noted that Crippen was to graduate at the end of the month. Dew found the Cleveland diploma when he searched 39 Hilldrop Crescent and, as David James Smith tells us in *Supper with the*

Crippens: 'The police would translate it into English, from Latin, just to be sure it was what it appeared to be. There was no doubt that Crippen was entitled to call himself Doctor.'

According to his account, following graduation Crippen worked as an assistant to a Dr Porter in Detroit for three or four months, then went to New York to train at the Ophthalmic Hospital, a homeopathic institution from which he graduated in 1885 with a qualification as an ear and eye specialist. With his poor memory for dates, Crippen cited a further two-year stint with Porter after his New York training but neglected to mention that he had at that time become engaged to Charlotte Jane Bell, a student nurse originally from Dublin. They were married in Detroit on 2 December 1887.

Early the next year the couple moved to San Diego, California — his parents were by then living in Los Angeles — where he opened a medical practice. Their only child, Hawley Otto, was born on 19 August 1889, and it must have been within a year or so of this date that the now iconic photograph of Dr Crippen was taken (see front cover). Large eyes peer out from behind small wire-rimmed glasses, and already the physical appearance that became famous twenty years later was clearly evident: thinning hair, high forehead and heavy moustache. The photograph does not reveal that he was only 5ft 4in tall.

By now well established in a pattern of regular relocation, Crippen moved his family to Salt Lake City, Utah, where Charlotte, aged about 33 and heavily pregnant, died suddenly in

January 1892 (not 1890 or 1891, as Crippen told Dew) from apoplexy — a stroke. There is no reason to suppose that her death was in any way unnatural, though a certain amount of later speculation was hardly avoidable in the circumstances.

This event started Crippen down the path that led eventually to the gallows. He sent Otto west to Los Angeles, where the boy remained until the death of his grandmother; father and son never again lived together. Crippen went east, back to New York, where he became an assistant to a Brooklyn doctor named Jeffery. Within months he met and married one of the two women around whom the rest of his life revolved.

CORA CRIPPEN

According to Crippen, he met Cora Turner when she visited Dr Jeffery as a patient; at his trial, he said he thought her illness was 'some miscarriage, or something of that kind'. This was certainly possible: despite her youth (she was born on 3 September 1873), Cora was no virgin. She was the mistress of a married New York stove manufacturer named C.C. Lincoln, with whom she had been living until he gave up his house and rented a room for her, paying her expenses and for singing lessons. Cora and Crippen took a liking to each other and began to spend time together. Eventually she told him that Lincoln wanted her to go away with him. As she had doubtless intended, Crippen immediately offered to make an honest woman of her.

They were married on 1 September 1892 in a Catholic ceremony in Jersey City (Cora was a practising Roman Catholic and eventually persuaded her husband to convert), and it was only some time after the wedding that she revealed her name was not Cora Turner but the rather less mellifluous Kunigunde Mackamotzki.

Cora Mackamotzki, as her family knew her, was the daughter of a Russian-Polish immigrant father who died young and a German mother, Mary. Cora's mother took as her second husband a Brooklyn farmer named Frederick (Fritz) Mersinger, with whom she had several more children. Strangely, the family was not invited to the wedding; Crippen met them for the first time a few days later. A photograph taken around that time (see plate 3) shows a group of 10 rather sullen-looking people: Cora, Crippen sporting an impressive spade beard, her mother and stepfather, and six children: two boys and four girls. The newlyweds look far more prosperous than the rest of the family.

Crippen got on well with Cora's family, but was rarely present in their lives as he travelled extensively in pursuit of work opportunities, never staying long in one place. Shortly after their wedding he and his wife moved to St Louis, where he worked for an optician, but they soon returned to New York. It was at about this time that a serious medical problem forced Cora to have surgery to remove her womb and ovaries, a procedure that left her barren and, as was later to prove crucial to the murder case against her husband, scarred. Her younger sister Theresa saw the scar shortly after the operation.

Cora greatly regretted not being able to become a mother. She offset her sorrow by continuing the singing lessons she loved, which Crippen was happy to pay for. The onset of an economic depression in May 1893, however, led to a financial pinch: the young couple were forced to move in with her parents. Larson suggests that it was the failure of his medical practice that led Crippen into the patent medicine business: it actually expanded during the depression because mail order remedies were cheaper than doctors'. One of the most successful companies in the business was Munyon's, with which Crippen had a long and profitable relationship.

James Munroe Munyon founded the Munyon Homeopathic Home Remedy Company in 1885. He established its headquarters in Philadelphia, from where he carried out an extremely lucrative trade in pills and potions alleged to 'cure' all manner of illnesses, including asthma, kidney problems, syphilis, scrofula, ulcers and haemorrhoids. With the advent of the 1906 Pure Food and Drug Act some of Munyon's preparations were analysed and found to contain few active ingredients: typical quack remedies, they were none the less profitable for that. Despite occasional ups and downs in their professional relationship, in 1910 the 'Professor' still thought well enough of Crippen to offer 250,000 German marks for his defence or as a reward to anyone who could prove that Cora Crippen was alive.

Crippen began working for Munyon in 1894 as a 'consulting

physician' in New York, and he and Cora moved out of Mersinger's house and into rooms above the office. After only a few months Crippen was transferred to Philadelphia, where he stayed a year before going to Toronto to manage the office there. Six months later he and Cora returned to Philadelphia, but by now she was tired of travelling in pursuit of his career; she wanted to renew her own musical ambition. Crippen told Dew that she decided to become an opera singer, and so, leaving him in Philadelphia, went to New York for voice training. Crippen was now earning enough to pay for singing lessons and accommodation, but it meant that the couple lived apart: in April 1897 Munyon sent him to England to manage the company's new branch on Shaftesbury Avenue at the alleged massive salary of $10,000.

Cora eventually joined him in August that year, having decided to abandon opera in favour of 'music hall sketches'. Crippen objected at first, but then decided to help: a playbill (reproduced in Jonathan Goodman's *The Crippen File*) named him as her manager. She had little success under the name Macka Motzki (his choice, not hers): an engagement at the Old Marylebone Music Hall ended after only a week, a humiliation that temporarily put her plans on hold. But when Crippen was called away to America in November 1899 she revived her musical ambitions, now using the stage name 'Belle Elmore'. Studio photographs taken at this time depict an attractive, dark-eyed, pouting brunette—and just the merest suggestion that she might one day run to fat (see plate 4).

When Crippen returned to London seven months later he noticed that something, or someone, had caused a change in their relationship. To make matters worse, he had been sacked by Munyon—who possibly feared he was launching a new career as an impresario—and needed to find another job.

THE ODD COUPLE

Always resourceful and by now committed to a career in patent medicines, Crippen worked as a manager or consulting physician to a number of impressively named but short-lived businesses. They were located in the vicinity of London's Marble Arch and Tottenham Court Road: the Sovereign Remedy Company, the Drouet Institute for the Deaf and the Aural Clinic Company. In 1905 he returned to Munyon's, which removed in May 1908 to Albion House in New Oxford Street; that same year he set himself up as an advertising agent called Franckel and started the Yale Tooth Specialist company with a New Zealand-trained dentist named Gilbert Rylance. When a quack named Scott Hamilton (aka Eddie Marr, who had taken over Drouet's in 1905) founded the Aural Remedies Company in September 1909, Crippen became its 'consulting specialist' (see plate 2).

Crippen also marketed himself as a specialist of the eye, throat and nose, and sold mail order remedies—including a nerve tonic and an ointment to cure deafness—from the flat he shared with Belle, as she now preferred to be known. This was in Store Street, where they had lived from June 1900 until they moved to 39 Hilldrop Crescent on 21 September 1905.

Despite its unremarkable character, Hilldrop Crescent was once the most famous street in England; number 39 the most infamous address in the world. The house was conveniently located. In 1906 the Camden Town tube station opened at the intersection of five busy streets, from where Camden Road ran north-east for more than a mile to Holloway Road. Halfway along, on the north side, it intersected the two ends of Hilldrop Crescent. The crescent's slightly shabby but respectable semi-detached houses were—in an arrangement unusual for London—numbered sequentially, and each had a built-to-impress flight of front door steps, a long back garden, a half basement and three floors above, giving ten or twelve rooms in all; some had greenhouses (see plate 1). The gardens at the southern end of the crescent were overlooked by the upstairs windows of houses in Brecknock Road; residents there noticed that the occupants of number 39 never drew down their upstairs blinds, nor raised the ones downstairs.

The neighbourhood was of mixed social status: Parmetes Row, a turning out of the crescent, was frequented by prostitutes. And by some ironic twist of fate, the crescent was sited uncomfortably close to not one prison but two: Pentonville lay to the east and Holloway was just a few hundred metres away, slightly to the north. Further to the west, the southern edge of Hampstead Heath was only fifteen minutes' brisk walk away.

The house was larger and more expensive than the Crippens needed — the annual rent was £52 10s, later £50 — but it had a beautiful garden. To save on costs, they lived in only a few rooms: the bedrooms on the top floor (they slept in separate rooms from the day they moved in), the kitchen and breakfast room in the basement. They initially took in three German lodgers, for company and income, who stayed for a year until Belle tired of the work they made for her; she did not keep a servant and had a charwoman in only occasionally. The house eventually fell into a state of semi-squalor, lacking light and ventilation according to her friend Adeline Harrison, whom Filson Young quotes extensively. The many pets — a number of birds, a couple of cats belonging to Belle, and a bull terrier of which Crippen was very fond — added to the general sense of disorder.

In the 1930s one of the lodgers, Karl Reinisch, gave a newspaper interview (MEPO 2/10996; see also plate 5) in which he remembered Crippen as extremely quiet and gentlemanly 'in thought and behaviour' to his wife and everyone else. He let her win at cards, made every effort to fulfil her wishes, and gave her a gramophone for Christmas. Belle was 'blonde, with a pretty face, of large, full, may I say of opulent figure'. Despite her theatrical ambitions she was a good housewife and an excellent cook.

Belle had some success in suburban and provincial music halls, but her talent never matched her ambition and she earned very little. She did, however, make many friends in minor theatrical circles, for she could be good company when she chose.

She and her husband, who was known to their mutual friends as 'Peter' (no one knows why), entertained regularly, and for two years before her death she was the honorary treasurer of a benevolent body called the Music Hall Ladies Guild. Crippen, who must have earned significantly more than his £3 per week salary from Munyon's, bought clothes, furs and jewellery to suit her extravagant tastes. At the end of January 1910 he was a few pounds overdrawn at the bank, but there was £600 on deposit, more than half in Belle's name.

The pretty, vivacious girl that Crippen had married became increasingly stout as the years went by, and her habit of bleaching her dark hair blonde must have effected quite an alteration in her appearance. Crippen, for his part, remained much the same as ever, though his sandy hair became scantier on top. A small man who neither drank nor smoked, his heavy moustache and protuberant eyes framed by gold-rimmed spectacles remained his most distinguishing features. Everyone who knew him agreed that he was kind, gentle and courteous; many recognized that he was dominated by his wife, who could at times be a sharp-tongued shrew. But he had a secret: he harboured a passion for another woman, and Belle knew it.

ETHEL LE NEVE

Ethel Neave—she later changed her surname to make it sound more middle class—was born on 22 January 1883 in Norfolk, the eldest of six children. The family moved to London when she was seven, and she decided to earn her own living as soon as she left school. She and her younger sister Nina trained as shorthand typists and took jobs at Drouet's in 1901, shortly before Crippen arrived. The three of them became good friends, and when Nina married in 1903, Ethel became Crippen's private secretary. When he returned to Munyon's, he took her with him.

Always rather poorly (by 1910 her colleagues knew her as the woman who regularly answered enquiries with the same remark, 'not very well, thank you'), Ethel found in Crippen a warm and sympathetic friend, and soon had him to thank for curing her of a long-term problem with catarrh. In *Her Life Story*, she recalled the mutual loneliness that brought them closer together: 'our friendship deepened almost inevitably. He used to come to see me at home. All this time his wife was shrouded in mystery.'

In 1904 Ethel encountered Mrs Crippen for the first time, and learned the reason for Crippen's reluctance to talk about her: on both occasions that Belle visited the office, angry words were exchanged. After a particularly traumatic incident when Ethel feared he had taken poison, Crippen told her that he could bear the ill-treatment no longer. They fell in love, and on 6 December 1906 they became lovers, Ethel's scruples having finally been overcome when she 'happened to see' some letters to Belle from Bruce Miller, a man who years later would have to deny in court that he had had an affair with her. Thereafter

Ethel and Crippen referred to each other in private moments as 'hub' and 'wifie'.

By all accounts a gentle and inoffensive girl, physically the opposite of Belle—neat, slender, ladylike and quiet—Ethel continued her affair with Crippen for years; in September 1908 she suffered a miscarriage. Belle seems to have foregone public displays of displeasure, although it is likely that she gave vent in private: visitors spoke of her nagging and outbursts of temper. Ethel, too, must have had moments of unhappiness: in Edwardian England, being the mistress of a married man was a precarious, socially perilous situation.

She may have used her friendship with John Stonehouse as a way of showing Crippen that she wanted the situation to change. Stonehouse was a chemist's clerk whom Ethel met when he moved into her lodging house in Hampstead at the end of January 1909, and they spent several weeks in company together until she disappeared to Brighton from March to August. When she returned to London, Crippen bought her a diamond ring, a welcome-home present and presumably an indication that their relationship was back on track. Stonehouse did not see her again after October.

This was the state of affairs at the end of 1909. Belle, the sharp-tongued bird of paradise, tolerated her husband; he was deeply in love with a woman who realized that affairs could not go on for ever. Perhaps they all recognized that sooner or later something would have to change.

CHAPTER ONE

The Lady Vanishes

On Monday 31 January 1910, rather late in the afternoon, Dr Crippen called at the home of his friends Paul and Clara Martinetti, retired music hall artists, to invite them to dinner that evening at 39 Hilldrop Crescent. They arrived at about 8 pm and the two couples ate in the breakfast room next to the kitchen. Belle cooked and served the meal, with some help from Mrs Martinetti. Afterwards they played cards. There was no sign of friction of any kind between the Crippens, and Belle was in good health and bright spirits when her guests left at 1.30 in the morning.

She was never seen or heard of again.

Dr Crippen, whose office was next door to that of the Music Hall Ladies Guild in Albion House, abruptly tendered his wife's resignation as treasurer in early February, and told its secretary she was leaving suddenly for America. Then on 20 February he brought his typist, Ethel Le Neve, to the Music Hall Benevolent Fund Dinner at the Criterion restaurant. The Martinettis and other friends by the name of Nash were shocked to see Ethel wearing some of Belle's diamonds. 'After watching their actions,' John Nash was later to say, 'I became very suspicious about Mrs Crippen's sudden disappearance' (T 1/11282/2913).

Several of Belle's theatrical friends tried to discover news of her, but nothing more happened until Nash and his wife, actress Lil Hawthorne, went to America towards the end of March and made enquiries there. While in New York they received a letter from Clara Martinetti saying that Peter Crippen had told her that Belle had died in Los Angeles. John Nash immediately contacted the police there via Mrs Ginnette, the president of the Music Hall Ladies Guild, and on 4 June he received a letter from Los Angeles saying that no person of that name had died there. When the Nashes returned to London on 23 June they met with various friends, who all doubted the story Crippen had told. In a last effort to get accurate information, Nash visited him on 28 June, to ask the name of the ship Belle had sailed on, where she had died and where she was cremated, but Crippen's odd behaviour and evasive answers convinced him 'that things were not what they should be' and he went to Scotland Yard on 30 June. He knew Superintendent Frank Froest, and made an appointment to see him two days later.

The Nashes then gave a statement to Froest, who months after the public furore had subsided commended their efforts in launching the case (T 1/11282/2913). Chief Inspector Walter Dew, an experienced detective who cut his teeth on the Jack the Ripper case in 1888, was asked to investigate. He had already learned some key points from the Nashes, information that gave him a good idea of where to begin.

Within a week Dew's enquiries revealed a long trail of suspicious circumstances leading back to the missing woman's husband. Taking Sergeant Arthur Mitchell with him, he first interviewed Melinda May, secretary to the Music Hall Ladies Guild. On 2 February, she told them, Ethel Le Neve had given her the Guild's bank books, along with two letters in Crippen's handwriting but signed 'Belle Elmore'. These explained her sudden resignation: 'Illness of a near relative has called me to America on only a few hours' notice… cannot spare a moment to call on you before I go.' On 23 March Crippen told her that Belle was very ill in America and that he was expecting a cable saying there was no hope for her. Since then, Miss May thought, he had been avoiding her.

When the Guild's committee heard of Belle's death they wrote to Crippen's son Otto in Los Angeles, asking for information. He replied on 9 May to say that the first he had heard of his stepmother's death was from his father, who told him she had died in San Francisco and that by mistake he had given out Otto's address as the place of death. Crippen had asked him to forward any letters he received, presumably with a view to answering them himself.

The police went on to interview other friends and associates of the Crippens. Dr John Burroughs and his wife Maud had been their neighbours in Store Street. Burroughs explained how, when he heard of Belle's death, he had written a letter of condolence. Crippen replied, informing him that Belle had died in California from pneumonia, having not told her husband how ill she was. He promised to visit soon, but never did.

The Martinettis told the officers about their dinner with the Crippens on 31 January. They had seen Crippen at noon the next day, when he said that Belle was 'all right'. When Crippen called on them a week later, however, Clara Martinetti rebuked him for not telling her about Belle's sudden departure. He told her they had been too busy packing for Belle to send a message. 'Packing and crying?' asked Mrs Martinetti. No, he replied, they had got over all that. Unusually for a woman of Belle's tastes she had—he said—taken only one basket of clothes; it was not enough but she could buy more. Over the next two weeks the Martinettis had received further visits and letters from Crippen, who described an increasingly serious bout of pneumonia but offered no explanation for why Belle did not contact her friends. On 23 March he told Mrs Martinetti that he hourly expected news of her death, and added, according to the trial testimony, 'If anything happens to Belle I shall go to France for a week'. Asked why, he said he could not stay in the house, and would need a change.

Crippen did go to France, but not alone. On 24 March he sent Mrs Martinetti a telegram from Victoria Station saying that Belle had died the day before and that he would be away for a week. Astounded, Mrs Martinetti went to see Dr Rylance, who could not offer any explanation but did say that Ethel Le Neve had also gone on her Easter holidays.

Clara Martinetti also reported how two weeks later she had seen Crippen again and asked if any of Belle's relatives were with her when she died. He said his son was, and that she had died in Los Angeles—the first time a location was offered. When asked which ship Belle had sailed on, Crippen replied that she went from Le Havre. Clara Martinetti had since seen Le Neve wearing some of Belle's furs. Paul Martinetti added that Crippen had told him that Belle had gone to America on legal business concerning a title to some land.

It was also discovered that on 26 March 1910 a death notice had appeared in *The Era*, a stage magazine (see plate 7).

These mysterious circumstances, plus the fact that Belle's friends could find no record that she had sailed on any ship, led Dew to investigate the couple's financial affairs. He discovered the joint account at the Charing Cross Bank and that Crippen had placed the death notice in *The Era*. In a report dated 6 July 1910 Dew concluded that the somewhat bohemian characters of the people involved meant that there was likely to be an explanation for the woman's disappearance, but that although the Crippens appeared to be a happy couple there were 'extraordinary contradictions' in the story the husband told (MEPO 3/198). It was not yet evident that foul play was involved, but it would be necessary to interview Mr Crippen.

AN INSPECTOR CALLS

At about 10 am on Friday 8 July Dew and Mitchell went to 39
Hilldrop Crescent, where a French maid let them in. She disappeared upstairs, and in a few minutes Ethel Le Neve came
down. Dew immediately noticed the distinctive rising sun
brooch she was wearing, and later discovered it had belonged to
Belle Elmore. Le Neve said that she was the housekeeper, and
became 'somewhat agitated' when Dew told her who they were.
As Crippen had gone to work she offered to go and fetch him,
expecting the police to come back later, but Dew insisted that
they go with her. The three of them went to Albion House, where
they found Crippen at the offices of the Yale Tooth Specialists.
Once he learned who they were and what they wanted, Crippen
must have realized that it was useless to persist in the story
about his wife's death, so he tried another approach: 'I suppose
I had better tell the truth. The stories I have told about her
death are untrue. As far as I know, she is still alive' (DPP 1/13).

At Dew's suggestion Crippen then made a long statement
in which he described his past, his wife and their marital unhappiness. He exuded confidence and a willingness to help. Dew
was impressed by his demeanour, but later interpreted this
misleading frankness as an indication that Crippen must have
expected a visit from the police sooner or later.

Crippen began giving his statement at noon. Dew occasionally interjected, while Mitchell wrote everything down in pencil.

According to Filson Young, Crippen darted in and out 'in the intervals between medical consultations and tooth-pulling'. They had not got very far in an hour. Not wanting to lose sight of him, Dew invited Crippen to lunch and along with Mitchell they went to an Italian restaurant nearby; Crippen tucked into a steak like a man without a worry in the world. On their return to Albion House, Crippen finished his statement at about 6 pm.

This document (CRIM 1/117; see plate 6) contains just enough truth to be convincing. After relating the story of his early life, Crippen described a woman who, practically as soon as she arrived in England, decided that he was not good enough for her because he compared unfavourably with 'the men of good position travelling on the boat who had made a fuss of her'. Not only did she cultivate a 'most ungovernable temper', but she sang at risqué venues ('smoking concerts') during his absence in Philadelphia and formed a close attachment to Bruce Miller, an American music hall artist whom she met in December 1899 and who had taken to visiting her regularly until his departure for Chicago in April 1904. Crippen said that he had not thought anything of Miller's visits, while hinting that there were grounds for suspicion. He also said that he had seen letters from Miller to Belle that ended 'with love and kisses to Brown Eyes'.

Crippen went on to explain that while he worked hard to fund Belle's lifestyle, the relationship broke down as her career foundered; they stopped sleeping together four years ago.

As I say she frequently threatened to leave me and said that if she did she would go right out of my life and I should never see or hear from her again.

On the Monday night, the day before I wrote the letter to the Guild, resigning her position as Treasurer, Mr and Mrs Paul Martinetti came to our place to dinner and during the evening Mr Martinetti wanted to go to the lavatory. As he had been to my house several times I did not take the trouble to go and show him where it was.

After they had left my wife blamed me for not taking him to the lavatory, and abused me and said 'This is the finish of it, I won't stand it any longer, I shall leave you tomorrow and you will never hear of me again.'

She had said this so often that I did not take much notice but she did say one thing which she had never said before, viz: I was to arrange to cover up any scandal with our mutual friends and the Guild the best way I could.

Before this she had told me frequently that the man she would go to was better able to support her than I was.

I came to business the next morning and when I went home between 5 and 6 pm I found she had gone.

He then described how he went about covering up her absence so as to prevent a scandal:

I think the same night or the next morning (Wednesday) I wrote a letter to the Guild saying she had gone away, which I also told several people.

I afterwards realized that this would not be a sufficient

explanation for her not coming back and later on I told people
that she was ill with bronchitis and pneumonia, and afterwards
I told them she was dead from this ailment.

I told them she died in California, but I have no recollection
of telling anyone exactly where she died.

Someone afterwards asked me where my son lived and I told
them.

I then put an advertisement in the *Era* that she was dead as I
thought this would prevent people asking me a lot of questions.

Whatever I have said to other people in regard to her death
is absolutely wrong and I am giving this as the explanation.

So far as I know she did not die and is still alive.

It is not true that she went away on legal business for me, or
to see any relatives in America.

I did not receive any cables to say she was ill, and it is not
true she was cremated at San Francisco and that the ashes
were sent to me, or that she sailed from Havre.

So far as I know she has no claim to any title.

I have no recollection of telling anyone my son was with her
when she died.

He described their joint finances and Belle's belongings:

We had a joint account at the Charing Cross Bank, subject to
the signature of either, but it pleased her to think she was
signing cheques, and she also did so, and several blank cheques
were always already signed by her, and some of these have
been changed by me since her departure and there is one here
now (produced).

When my wife went away I cannot say if she took anything with her or not, but I believe there is a theatrical travelling basket missing and she might have taken this with some clothes.

She took some of her jewellery I know with her, but she left four rings behind—three single stone (or Solitaire) diamond and a four diamonds and a ruby one, also a diamond brooch.

She had other jewellery and must have taken this with her.

I have never pawned or sold anything belonging to her before or after she left.

… I do not know what clothes, if any, she took away, she had plenty.

Whenever we quarrelled and she threatened to leave me, she told me she wanted nothing from me.

I have bought all her jewellery and so far as I know, she never had any jewellery presents, and I do not know that she ever had any money sent her except that Bruce Miller used to send her small amounts on her birthday and at Easter and Christmas to purchase a present.

Crippen then mentioned that Belle had suffered from bilious attacks, saying that he had given her homeopathic remedies for them. He went on to describe his relationship with Ethel Le Neve:

Miss Le Neve has been in my employ and known by me through being employed by the firms I have worked for, for the past eight years, and she is now living with me as my wife at Hilldrop Crescent. I have been intimate with her during the past three years and have frequently stayed with her at hotels, but never was away from home at night.

> After I told people my wife was dead Miss Le Neve and I
> went to Dieppe for about 5 days, and stayed at an hotel there (I
> forget the name, but the proprietor's name was Vacher) in the
> name of Mr and Mrs Crippen.

Crippen ended by speculating that his wife had gone to Chicago
to join Miller, and by reiterating his readiness to help the police.

He then read the statement through carefully, initialled each
page and signed at the end: he had freely admitted to being a
liar and offered, as he thought, a new yet plausible explanation
for his wife's disappearance. Dew later recalled thinking that
he would need to probe further, as 'you can't charge a man with
being a liar', but first he asked Ethel Le Neve for her account of
the affair. Her statement (CRIM 1/117), also dictated to Sergeant
Mitchell, included the following words:

> Since the latter end of February I have been living at 39 Hill-
> drop Crescent with Mr Crippen as his wife.
>
> … I have been on intimate terms with Mr Crippen for between
> two and three years, but I have known him for 10 years.
>
> I made his acquaintance by being in the same employ as he.
>
> I knew Mrs Crippen and have visited at Hilldrop Crescent.
> She treated me as a friend.
>
> In the early part of February I received a note from Mr
> Crippen saying Mrs Crippen had gone to America and asking
> me to hand over a packet he enclosed to Miss May.
>
> About 4 pm same day he came to our business place, Albion
> House, and told me his wife had gone to America. He said she

had packed up and gone.

I had been in the habit for the past 2 or 3 years of going about with him, and continued doing so.

About a week after he told me she had gone to America I went to Hilldrop Crescent to put the place straight as there were no servants kept, but at night time I went to my lodgings; and I did this daily for about a fortnight. The place appeared to be all right, and quite as usual.

He took me to the Benevolent Fund Dinner and lent me a brooch (diamond) to wear and later on he told me I could keep it.

After this he told me she had caught a chill on board the ship and had got pneumonia, and afterwards he told me she was dead.

He told me he could not go to the funeral as it was too far and she would have been buried before he could get there.

Before he ever told me this I had been away with him for five or six days at Dieppe and stayed at a hotel with him in the names of Mr and Mrs Crippen, but I cannot tell you the name of the place.

When we came back he took me to Hilldrop Crescent and I remained there with him, occupying the same bedroom. The same night or the night after he told me that Belle was dead. I was very much astonished, but I don't think I said anything to him about it.

I have not had any conversation with him about it since.

He gave me some furs of his wife's to wear, and I have been living with him ever since as his wife and have given up my lodgings at Constantine Road and taken up my abode at Hilldrop Crescent.

My father and mother do not know what I am doing and think I am a housekeeper at Hilldrop Crescent.

When Mr Crippen told me his wife had gone to America I don't remember if he told me she was coming back or not.

I cannot remember if he went into mourning.

Ethel appeared slightly embarrassed at admitting to an affair with a married man, but otherwise seemed to have nothing to hide. Their statements supplied, the couple returned to Hilldrop Crescent with the police. At Crippen's invitation the officers looked around the house, including the cellar and garden, but saw nothing suspicious. On being told that Dew would have to find Mrs Crippen before he could end the inquiry, Crippen offered to write an advertisement for the American newspapers: 'Mackamotzki: Will Belle Elmore communicate with H. H. C. or authorities at once. Serious trouble through your absence. $25 reward to any one communicating her whereabouts to —'.

The detectives left after 8 pm, apparently satisfied with what they had seen and heard, but the next day Dew circulated every police station in London with a description of Mrs Crippen as a missing person. He spent the rest of the weekend mulling over the case, and on the morning of Monday 11 July he returned to Albion House intending to ask Crippen more questions. 'Then came the bombshell,' Dew later recalled in his memoir *I Caught Crippen*. 'Crippen had flown. Miss Le Neve was also missing. Pretty obvious the couple had gone away together.' It was time to find out why.

FLIGHT

On the morning of 9 July Crippen went to Albion House much earlier than usual. Ethel turned up later, having first gone to visit her sister, Nina Brock. Neither of them had any luggage. William Long, a dental technician who had known and worked with Crippen for over a decade, was surprised to see him so early and asked if there was any trouble, to which Crippen replied, 'Only a little scandal' (quoted at trial). He then sent Long out to buy a list of boy's clothes: a brown tweed suit, brown felt hat, two shirts, two collars, a tie, and a pair of boots. Gilbert Rylance was also in the office and spoke to Crippen at about noon. Marion Curnow, who had succeeded Crippen as Munyon's manager on 1 February, cashed a cheque for £37 for him. No one saw Crippen or Le Neve after 1 pm.

That evening Rylance and Long received letters from Crippen. Long's, postmarked at 4.15 pm, asked him to 'wind up my household affairs' and enclosed his door key. To Rylance, Crippen wrote that 'to escape trouble I shall be obliged to absent myself for a time' (quoted at trial); he handed over the business for the dentist to continue as he pleased. These letters were given to Dew when he arrived on Monday morning, after which he went back to Scotland Yard to discuss the development with Froest.

Dew and Mitchell set off for Hilldrop Crescent that afternoon. Mrs Flora Long was already there with the maid, Valentine

Lecocq, who had only worked in the house for a month and could shed no light on the disappearance of her employer. Mrs Long had just pawned some women's clothes to raise money to pay the rent (which Crippen had asked her to do), and found the draft advertisement seeking information about Belle abandoned under a sofa. Her husband arrived later and told the police that he had discovered Ethel's hat and Crippen's suit hidden in a cupboard at Albion House. In his formal report on the events of 8–13 July (DPP 1/13) Dew commented testily:

> The point I ought to emphasize concerning this matter is that I saw Long on Monday 11th and Tuesday 12th, but it was not until Wednesday morning—13th—when I told him that I thought he knew more than he had told me, that he mentioned one word about purchasing a boy's suit etc for Crippen on the Saturday.

Dew and Mitchell spent the rest of 11 July making a further 'very careful search of the house and grounds', including a cursory look round the cellar, but failed to find anything suspicious apart from a loaded revolver in a wardrobe, a box of cartridges and some cardboard targets in the kitchen. Dew then circulated information about Crippen to ports at home and abroad, and tried to find out if any boxes or packages had been removed from the house since 31 January. The next day he and Mitchell returned to Hilldrop Crescent to ask more questions around the neighbourhood, but again failed to find anything useful. The fact that Crippen had fled pointed to guilt, but what exactly was he guilty of?

CHAPTER TWO

Torso in the Cellar

It was not until 13 July, four days after Crippen vanished, that Dew and Mitchell 'dug several parts of the garden, and finally went to the coal cellar again, the flooring of which was brick' (MEPO 3/198; see plates 8–11). The cellar, which was under the front steps, was reached by a short passage which led from the kitchen to the back door. The policemen got down on hands and knees and examined the floor, then took a small poker and probed the brickwork until a loose brick was dislodged. The others came up easily, and Dew then dug into the clay beneath — to find what he suspected were human remains.

He sent to Kentish Town police station for help, and PCs Daniel Gooch and Frederick Martin arrived to assist in the gruesome task of excavating the remains, which were buried six to eight inches deep. They dug until 11 pm. The terrible smell hindered their work, but they had soon unearthed a large mass of what Dew immediately took to be flesh. He sent for the Assistant Police Commissioner, Sir Melville Macnaghten, and the local police surgeon, Dr Thomas Marshall.

Marshall arrived at Hilldrop Crescent at 5.30 pm 'and saw human remains exposed in the earth of the front cellar'. He left after about an hour, but returned at 9.15 when the remains were more clearly revealed. A photograph of the grave does not do justice to the impact it must have made: the indistinct mass did not look much like a body, but the stench told another story. Marshall examined what he could without touching anything, and observed that there were 'internal organs displayed on the top'. The next day he and the Home Office pathologist, Dr Pepper, oversaw their removal to a crude coffin by Gooch and Martin, who used their bare hands despite the disgusting odour.

Who could doubt that this was the secret Crippen had been hiding? But Dew recalled in his memoirs that suspicion and surmise were not enough. It was his job to get the proof:

> First, it had to be established that the remains were those of a woman. Next, that the woman was Belle Elmore. Thirdly that it was a case of murder, and finally, if murder had been done, that Crippen had committed the deed. The first problem was settled by the doctors.

HUMAN REMAINS

At about 11 am on Thursday 14 July Dew returned to Hilldrop Crescent with Augustus Joseph Pepper, a consultant surgeon from St Mary's Hospital, Paddington. Pepper was to become one of the prosecution's chief medical witnesses in the case against Crippen: no mere surgeon, he was a highly experienced forensic pathologist who had become famous when he used dental records to identify a missing murder victim (the Moat Farm murder of 1903), and who had been the official Home Office pathologist since the 1890s. Macnaghten had instructed him to examine the remains, and Pepper was soon joined in the case by his St Mary's colleagues, William Willcox and Bernard Spilsbury. Again, this was no accident: St Mary's has been described as the birthplace of modern English forensic medicine. Apart from the pathologist Pepper and his junior Spilsbury (who was to become the greatest of the 'medical detectives'), there were the toxicologists Willcox and Arthur Luff, the latter having resigned the post of Home Office analyst in 1904 (on which he became honorary scientific adviser to the Home Office) in favour of his junior, Willcox, who held the post of senior analyst until 1919. This formidable team of experts — all of whom worked tirelessly to prove the case against Crippen — was virtually unassailable in its authority and influence.

When they arrived at Hilldrop Crescent, Pepper already knew that a woman had disappeared around the end of January, and during the course of the three hours he spent there he learned that the woman in question was stout, in early middle age and had been on the music hall stage. A case could therefore be made that he went into the investigation with preformed ideas, but in fact the evidence really did speak for itself. Dew continued his search of the house, which soon yielded another vital clue: a box found under a bed contained two pairs of pyjamas and a single pair of pyjama trousers. The likely fate of its partner jacket was to become evident once Pepper began a close examination of the contents of the grave.

Pepper was joined in this preliminary examination by Dr Marshall. The record of his findings shows that his first impression was that part of the cellar floor had been dug up to expose 'animal remains' which occupied a space roughly the length and breadth of a human body. The soil was made up of loam and clay, with some 'lime' mixed up in it. Near one end of the remains some objects were found and put into a tray: a tuft of dark brown hair in a Hinde's curler (Marshall later found two more coated in earth and lime); a small piece of short fair hair in a tattered, man's size white handkerchief, two corners of which were tied in a reef knot; and part of what appeared to be a woman's camisole with six pearly buttons, a lace collar and armlets. There was also a large piece of flesh — skin, fat and muscle — which appeared to come from the upper part of a thigh. By the time all this had been extracted from the cellar floor, Pepper was certain that he was dealing with human remains.

He made a quick examination at the house before the remains were taken to the Islington mortuary, where he examined them the next day, 15 July. The coroner, Dr Danford Thomas, had asked him to conduct the formal autopsy, with Marshall's assistance. It would usually have been the job of the police surgeon to conduct an autopsy, and the fact that

Pepper took the lead is another indication of how significant the authorities considered the case. Dew, Mitchell and the mortuary 'keeper' Arthur Robinson were present throughout.

It was here that the full extent of the butchery became evident: all the bones had been removed, the head and limbs — apart from a piece of thigh — were missing, and there was no trace of genitals or evidence of sex, though there was a line of what he thought were pubic hairs along one piece of flesh. The internal organs were, however, nearly complete, and were found in one continuous mass: liver, stomach (empty), gullet, lower part of the windpipe, two lungs, heart, pancreas, diaphragm, both kidneys, spleen, all the small intestines and most of the large. Their size, together with the muscular development of the five large and several smaller chunks of flesh from the chest and back, indicated that what was found in the cellar at 39 Hilldrop Crescent corresponded to the torso of — judging by the fat around the heart — a rather stout adult.

When Pepper testified two months later at the committal proceedings at Bow Street police court (a preliminary process to determine whether the accused should be committed for trial), he pointed out that:

> It would not be a difficult thing to remove all this mass in one part from the body, but it would be a difficult thing to do it as it was done. There was no cut or tear in any of the viscera, except where it was necessary for removal [i.e. at the gullet and large intestine]. (DPP 1/13)

The person who did it must have had enough knowledge of human or animal anatomy to know exactly where to cut and pull. At the trial, in answer to the judge, Pepper avoided stating positively that the butcher was skilled in 'dissection', which implied experience in cutting up human bodies, but stressed that whoever dismembered the body must have had experience of eviscerating animals. The prosecution never really proved that Crippen had the necessary experience, but let the jury assume that his medical qualification meant that he must ('if a person had once learned how to do it, he could do it', said Pepper).

Instead, the approach was to establish Crippen's guilt by association. If the body was that of his wife, they reasoned, who else could have killed her? One of the large pieces of flesh from the lower abdomen, measuring six inches by seven, had a mark on it that, in the opinion of the prosecution and their medical experts, corresponded to a scar. Not just any scar, but a scar in the precise location where one would be found on a woman who had had her ovaries removed. As, of course, Mrs Crippen had.

Although this was to prove the most damning evidence against Crippen—and it is explored more fully later in this chapter—it was not the only thing that could help to establish the identity of the body and its killer. Pepper discovered, on closer examination of the remains excavated from the cellar, parts of a pyjama jacket, including the collar, which helpfully had a label identifying the maker as Jones Brothers Limited, of Holloway. However, no further information about the pyjama jacket's maker was obtained until Crippen's trial had actually begun. In July and August, the police were more concerned with finding Crippen and Le Neve, while the medical experts continued to scrutinize the body parts.

Pepper began his close examination with the hair found in the grave, which was of various shades of brown. He quickly realized that its natural colour was dark brown, but that the lighter colours were due to 'gradations of bleaching', the palest colour being quite 'yellow'. Given the length of the hairs found—the longest were eight inches—and the fact that they had been bleached, he decided that they must have belonged to a woman. The darkest parts came from closest to the scalp, and the roots were present (wig hair would be cut at both ends). Over the following weeks the bleached part of the hair was to darken, so that when the police court sat at Bow Street in September it had only Pepper's testimony, corroborated by Dr Marshall, as to its blonde colour when exhumed.

By this time Pepper had been able to examine the two further hanks of hair found by Marshall on 25 July and 14 August, both of which had been curled up in Hinde's hairpins. A patented product (the company was based in Finsbury) made with a hard rubber stem and wire frame, the hairpins were three to four inches long and of a type used regularly by thousands of women, including Belle Elmore. Finally, the absence of grey hair gave a clue to the victim's age. The evidence from the hair was thus strongly suggestive of a young or middle-aged female victim, who had bleached her dark hair—'a man often dyes his grey hair black, but does not bleach it,' said Pepper (DPP 1/13).

Pepper then turned his attention to the internal organs, all of which seemed to be healthy and fairly well preserved; the lungs and spleen had begun to decompose, but there was absolutely no evidence of any disease that might account for death. He was certain that the remains had been buried for between four and eight months, and could not have been in the cellar for as long as a year, because the body parts would not then have been found in such good condition. In his opinion burial had taken place soon after death because there was

> so little of the common or usual form in which putrefaction affects dead bodies and because of the decided evidence of another process of decay, i.e. the formation of a soap, the technical name is adipocere. That is what I should expect to find in the case of a body buried soon after death, buried in the condition of the ground in which this body was found. (DPP 1/13)

Those conditions included the depth (six to eight inches beneath the brick floor), and the presence of clay and lime. The lime was an important point, as it explained the current state of decomposition of the flesh. Although this was never discussed in any detail, it is clear that the 'lime' found in the grave was slaked lime, calcium hydroxide, which had set into hard lumps that would have no discernible effect on the remains; if it had been quicklime (calcium oxide) it would have tended to retard decomposition in these damp conditions though in drier conditions it could destroy flesh by caustic action.

Marshall added that the presence of adipocere convinced him that there had been a period of several months since burial. Adipocere, a smelly brownish-white waxy substance formed from decomposing body fat, develops most quickly in moist airless environments, a process that takes about three months in an average English climate.

At Bow Street and at the trial Pepper was to be cross-examined as to the length of time the remains might have been buried. He stuck to his estimate of four to eight months, admitting only that science could not accurately determine the time since death on the basis of putrefaction, and that different bodies might react differently under identical conditions. Pepper's certainty that the remains could not have been buried as long as a year was another strong piece of evidence against Crippen: the grave must have been filled while he occupied 39 Hilldrop Crescent, making his claim that they could have been buried there before he moved in on 21 September 1905 an absurd impossibility.

Even in the absence of anatomical evidence of gender, it was looking more and more likely that the body buried in the cellar was that of Crippen's wife. To establish this beyond any possible doubt, the prosecution had to focus on the piece of skin with the curious mark on it. Pepper led the attack. Up to this point the defence team had raised few questions about his evidence, but this was about to change.

SCAR OR FOLD?

It is not clear what Pepper was doing between 15 July and 8 August, when he went back to the mortuary with Marshall. He might have been on holiday, as the coroner, Dr Thomas, was (he died suddenly in Hastings in early August, and his deputy, Walter Schröder, took over responsibility for the inquest, which ran in parallel with the proceedings at Bow Street). This second visit, however, was to be absolutely critical to the case against Crippen, for it was then that both Pepper and Marshall noticed that one of the pieces of skin from the abdomen, measuring seven inches by six (the longer measurement represented the length from the lower portion of the abdomen upwards), held a mark that merited closer attention.

This mark, mainly vertical but slightly curving to the left at its upper end, was about four inches long, seven-eighths of an inch wide at the bottom, half an inch in the middle, and a quarter of an inch at the top. It was darker than the surrounding skin, lacked sebaceous glands, and had many fine lines running across it from edge to edge, strongly suggesting that it was scar tissue; its width showed that it had stretched after healing. At the bottom, Pepper found twenty hairs, from half an inch to an inch long, dark brown with roots at one end and tapered at the other; microscopic examination proved that they were pubic hairs. Their presence demonstrated that the scar was originally positioned on the lower middle of the abdomen, and its colour and size indicated that it was an old surgical wound, the pigmentation having probably resulted from slow healing and subsequent stretching.

There was no navel. Pepper thought it had probably been removed at the time of the operation—a common practice, apparently, to make it easier to keep the wound clean. Pepper was later to claim that he realized the mark was a scar within fifteen minutes of looking closely at it, but admitted that within a week of first seeing the remains he had heard that Belle Elmore had had an operation. The information came from Marshall via Dew, who overheard Clara Martinetti talking about it after the inquest on 18 July.

Following his examination on 8 August Pepper took the section of skin to Willcox, who preserved what was *the* critical piece of evidence in a solution of formalin. It was closely inspected by more doctors the following month, because it was potentially ambiguous, not being simply a flat piece of skin with a clearly defined scar on it: when it was excavated from the cellar, it was folded over on itself from the pressure of the clay and other materials on top of it. In fact, its fat had been removed so that it could fold over, and when the skin was laid out flat a groove along the line of the scar was visible—but Pepper categorically denied that this groove was caused solely by folding. The actual fold was not along the line of the scar at all, but formed a kind of crescent around the upper end of the skin quite distinct from the scar; this was to become known as the left limb of the horseshoe mark, the right limb being part of the scar.

This issue, in the hands of a skilful defence lawyer, had the potential to undermine the prosecution case, which of course rested on the fact that the alleged victim had a scar in just the position the medical experts had claimed to find one. This was, literally, the ground over which the battle for Crippen's life was fought. The skin was brought into court and scrutinized by the jury: the arguments were highly complicated, so much so that during the trial the judge had to admit 'I do not quite understand what has been put to you.'

In the absence of clear photographs of the key piece of flesh, it is important to sketch the gist of the arguments made by the prosecution and the defence. The prosecution knew from the middle of July that Belle Elmore had an abdominal scar from an old operation (see plate 14), and claimed that they had found it on a piece of skin buried in the cellar at 39 Hilldrop Crescent. The defence first tried to prove that the skin was not from an abdomen but a buttock: the presence of abdominal muscles and pubic hairs disproved this. They then pounced on the claim that the navel had been removed. But Belle was known to have had hers and Pepper had to revise his opinion that navel removal was the norm among surgeons who performed hysterectomies.

Finally they tried to show that the scar was not a scar at all, but merely a fold mark. To do this, the defence knew they needed to fight fire with fire: they had to bring in their own medical experts. Accordingly, on 9 September the flesh was

1 *Above*: 39 Hilldrop Crescent: the murder house. (MEPO 3/198)

2 *Left*: Dr Crippen's business circular for the Aural Remedies Company, for which he was 'consulting specialist'. (COPY 1/550)

F. MERSINGER AND HIS FAMILY

① DR. H. H. CRIPPEN ② MRS. H. H. CRIPPEN ③ MRS. CRIPPEN'S MOTHER ④ F. MERSINGER (MRS. CRIPPEN'S STEP FATHER)

DR. CRIPPEN'S SIGNATURE

3 *Above*: The Crippens with Cora's family, the Mersingers, taken around the time of their marriage. (DPP 1/13)

4 *Top right*: Studio portrait of Cora Crippen. (MEPO 3/198)

5 *Right*: Letter written from Cora Crippen to Karl Reinisch; it shows something of her pleasant but grandiose personality. (MEPO 3/198)

6 *Right*: Pages from Crippen's police statement of 8 July 1910; he denied all knowledge of his wife's whereabouts. (CRIM 1/117)

7 *Below*: The notice of Belle's (Cora's) death in California, 26 March 1910, that Crippen supplied to *The Era*. (CRIM 1/117)

Exhibit 9 No:

(8)

8th July 1910.
Albion House
New Oxford St.

name of Mr and Mrs Crippen.

My belief is that my wife has gone to Chicago to join Bruce Miller, whose business on the Music Hall Stage is a Musical Instrument turn, but I think he has now gone into another business and has speculated and made money. Mr Didcot was his agent when he was over here.

I shall, of course, do all I can to get in touch with her so as to clear this matter up.

She has a sister named Louise whose name is Mills, living with her husband, who is a Soap maker, I think living at Brooklyn - in fact I know living there. They live with my wife's stepfather Mr Maßsangar.

I do not know where any of her other relations live. I cannot tell you how to find or trace her, except as I have already said.

I will willingly go to my house with you to see if I can find any letters which may throw any light on the matter, and I invite you to look round the house and do whatever you like in the house.

This is all I can tell you.

Any notes that I have changed through anyone in this building were in connection with my business.

This statement has been read over to me. It is quite correct and has been made by me quite voluntarily and without any promise or threat having been held out to me.

Hawley Harvey Crippen.
July 8th 1910.

Walter Dew.
Chf Inspr.
8th July 1910.

Witness.

DEATHS.
ARCHER.—On Thursday, March 17, 1910, at the Royal Infirmary, Liverpool, Marie Pritchard, the beloved wife of Frederick Archer, of "Two Little Vagabonds" Co. "Into Thy Hands, O Lord."
ELMORE.—March 23, in California, U.S.A., Miss Belle Elmore (Mrs. H. H. Crippen).
Fox.—March 4, at Utica, N.Y., Imro Fox, magician, aged 60.
HALL.—Feb. 8, at Sydney, N.S.W., Mrs. George

On Tuesday, 12th, with Sergeant Mitchell, I made further careful examination of 39 Hilldrop Crescent, and made various enquiries.

On Wednesday, 13th, I made enquiries in various directions and endeavoured to trace boxes said to have been removed from 39 Hilldrop Crescent, and again, with Sergeant Mitchell, went to that address and again dug several parts of the garden, and finally went to the Coal cellar again, the flooring of which was brick.

We went down on our hands and knees and carefully examined the brick flooring again, but everything appeared to be in order.

We then got a small poker and tested various parts of the flooring of the basement and probed about the brickwork of the cellar, and in doing so the poker, which has a thin point, went in between two of the bricks, which became loosened, and Sergeant Mitchell and I then removed several bricks and found underneath a flat surface of clay.

I then procured a spade from the garden and dug, and on taking the surface up we found the earth somewhat loose, and after digging about three spade fulls I came across what appeared to be human flesh, but on account of the terrible smell, we had to cease our labours for a time.

On resuming the digging we unearthed a large mass of flesh, and then sent for the Divisional Surgeon

8 *Left*: Chief Inspector Walter Dew's statement describing the police search of Crippen's house beginning on 13 July 1910. (MEPO 3/198)

9 *Above*: The police team who searched 39 Hilldrop Crescent: Walter Dew is on the right. (MEPO 3/198)

12 *Right*: Police 'Wanted' poster for Crippen and le Neve, 16 July 1910. (MEPO 3/198)

10 *Above*: Interior of Crippen's home taken after the police search. (MEPO 3/198)

11 *Right*: The police excavations in the cellar; here human flesh was found. (MEPO 3/198)

METROPOLITAN POLICE

MURDER

AND MUTILATION.

**Portraits, Description and Specimen of Handwriting of HAWLEY
HARVEY CRIPPEN, alias Peter Crippen, alias Franckel; and
ETHEL CLARA LE NEVE, alias Mrs. Crippen, and Neave.**

Wanted for the Murder of CORA CRIPPEN, otherwise Belle
Elmore; Kunigunde Mackamotzki; Marsangar and Turner, on,
or about, 2nd February last.

Description of Crippen.—Age 50, height 5 ft. 3 or 4,
complexion fresh, hair light brown, inclined sandy, scanty, bald on
top, rather long scanty moustache, somewhat straggly, eyes grey, bridge
of nose rather flat, false teeth, medium build, throws his feet outwards
when walking. May be clean shaven or wearing a beard and gold
rimmed spectacles, and may possibly assume a wig.

Sometimes wears a jacket suit, and at other times frock coat
and silk hat. May be dressed in a brown jacket suit, brown hat and
stand up collar (size 15).

Somewhat slovenly appearance, wears his hat rather at back of head
Very plausible and quiet spoken, remarkably cool and collected
demeanour.

Speaks French and probably German. Carries Firearms.

An American citizen, and by profession a Doctor.

Has lived in New York, Philadelphia, St. Louis, Detroit, Michigan,
Coldwater, and other parts of America.

May obtain a position as assistant to a doctor or eye specialist,
or may practise as an eye specialist, Dentist, or open a business for the
treatment of deafness, advertising freely.

Has represented Munyon's Remedies, in various cities in America.

Description of Le Neve alias Neave.—A shorthand writer
and typist, age 27, height 5 ft. 5, complexion pale, hair light brown
(may dye same), large grey or blue eyes, good teeth, nice looking,
rather long straight nose (good shape), medium build, pleasant, lady-like
appearance. Quiet, subdued manner, talks quietly, looks intently when
in conversation. A native of London.

Dresses well, but quietly, and may wear a blue serge costume (coat reaching to hips) trimmed heavy braid, about
¾ inch wide, round edge, over shoulders and pockets. Three large braid buttons down front, about size of a florin, three
small ones on each pocket, two on each cuff, several rows of stitching round bottom of skirt; or a light grey shadow-stripe
costume, same style as above, but trimmed grey moire silk instead of braid, and two rows of silk round bottom of skirt;
or a white princess robe with gold sequins; or a mole coloured striped costume with black moire silk collar; or a dark
vieuxrose cloth costume, trimmed black velvet collar; or a light heliotrope dress.

May have in her possession and endeavour to dispose of same:—a round gold brooch, with points radiating zig-zag from
centre, each point about an inch long, diamond in centre, each point set brilliants, the brooch in all being slightly larger
than a half-crown; and two single stone diamond rings, and a diamond and sapphire (or ruby) ring, stones rather large.

Absconded 9th inst. and may have left, or will endeavour to leave the country.

Please cause every enquiry at Shipping Offices, Hotels, and other likely places, and cause ships to be watched.

Information to be given to the Metropolitan Police Office, New Scotland Yard, London, S.W., or at any Police Station.

E. R. HENRY,
The Commissioner of Police of the Metropolis.

Metropolitan Police Office,
New Scotland Yard. 16th July, 1910.

13 *Right*: Ethel le Neve posing in boy's clothes, *Lloyd's Weekly News*, 20 November 1910. (PCOM 8/30)

14 *Below*: Letter from Inspector J. Russell of New York to Scotland Yard, 22 July 1910: it refers to Cora's operation being potentially useful for identification. (MEPO 3/198)

NOV. 20. 1910.

LLOYD'S WEEKLY

DR. CRIPPEN.

FAREWELL MESSAGE THROUGH "LLOYD'S NEWS."

MISS LE NEUE.

We have received the following message from Dr. Crippen, through Miss Le Neve, with the request that it should be published in "Lloyd's News":—

PENTONVILLE PRISON.

This is my farewell letter to the world. After many days of anxious expectation that my innocence might be proved, after enduring the agony of a long trial and the suspense of an appeal, and after the final endeavour of my friends to obtain, a reprieve, I see that at last my doom is sealed and that in this life I have no more hope.

With all the courage I have I face another world and another Judge—from Whom I am sure of justice greater than that of this world and of mercy greater than that of men.

I have no dread of death, no fear of the hereafter, only the dread and the agony that one where I live believing suffer when I have gone. Death, I say, has no terror for me, and I fear not at all the passing from this life. I am powerful now, and fear to the inevitable.

But in this letter of farewell I desire to make a last appeal to the world and to think the worst of me, and to believe words now written from the condemned cell...

examined at the behest of the defence solicitor, Arthur Newton, by Dr Gilbert Turnbull, director of the Pathological Institute at the London Hospital and an experienced pathologist and micro-scopist, and Dr Reginald Wall, an assistant physician to the London Hospital and until recently one of its pathologists. On this first occasion Turnbull said little to Pepper other than to ask whether he had 'microscoped' the scar. Until then, remark-ably, Pepper had not thought it necessary to do so. He now removed a piece of the preserved flesh for Bernard Spilsbury, who saw it for the first time that day and later removed two more sections, one from the right edge of the specimen and the other from a fold in the skin near the left edge. He was able to distinguish the remains of sebaceous glands in the pieces from both edges, but not in the middle where the mark was.

Colin Evans's new biography of Spilsbury, *The Father of Forensics*, points out that just two years before the Crippen case he had published research on the scarring of human skin, and therefore knew 'as much as anyone alive' about the subject. So it was with a practised eye that Spilsbury studied the mark and came to the conclusion that it was an old scar. Microscopical examination confirmed this opinion and revealed a dense texture and lack of glands, proving that the scar had been stretched. At both the police court proceedings and the trial the defence implied that Spilsbury was merely repeating the infor-mation his boss, Pepper, wanted to hear. Spilsbury countered this authoritatively: 'I have an independent position of my own, and I am responsible for my own opinion, which has been formed on my own scientific knowledge.' As earlier biographers Browne and Tullett noted, 'Here was a new, dominating voice in the courts of justice.'

Doctors Wall and Turnbull, meanwhile, had concluded that the mark could not possibly be a scar or come from the abdomen, and said so at Bow Street. They did not realize that they would be called as defence witnesses at the trial until the week before it began; however, Newton, a brilliant maverick, had asked them to sign a report, which meant that they became official witnesses in the case and could not refuse to testify. Once they received this worrying news they returned to St Mary's to study the piece of flesh again on 15 and 17 October, delaying only long enough to read through the evidence that Pepper, Spilsbury and Willcox had given at Bow Street (neither had been present during their testimony). The records now in the National Archives do not include the defence documents, so we have only the trial testimony to tell us their opinions on the mark.

This indicates that after they viewed the flesh in October, Wall and Turnbull recognized that it probably did come from the abdomen, but held firm to the view that the mark upon it was not a scar: microscopical examination had revealed five hair follicles and a sebaceous gland, which could not exist in a true scar. It must, therefore, be a fold. In fact, Spilsbury realized that a small flap of skin had been folded under as the scar healed, and this was the source of the hairs. Years later, Browne and Tullett reveal, Spilsbury told a friend that Turnbull became aware he had been tricked into testifying and telephoned him for advice. Spilsbury recommended that he withdraw the report, but Turnbull decided to stand by it. That was a mistake: he and Wall were humiliated by the fractious judge and imperious senior counsel for the prosecution.

Although Pepper (who devoted 24 hours in total to examining the body parts) and Spilsbury were able to provide strong evidence that the remains were those of Belle Elmore, they could not say how she died. If it was murder, it had to be proved; cutting up and burying a dead body, though unusual and objectionable, was not a capital offence. They needed to know the cause of death, so they turned to William Willcox.

HYOSCINE

On 15 July an assortment of samples from the grave were placed in five glass jars and sealed by Marshall and Pepper. They remained at the mortuary under the care of Arthur Robinson until 22 July, when he gave them to the coroner's officer, PC Robert Thompson, who delivered them to Willcox in his laboratory at St Mary's. The delay was caused by the fact that the coroner had to seek permission from the Home Office to call in its official analyst, which he did on 20 July.

The first jar contained the heart, the stomach (attached to a considerable amount of fat), one kidney and a piece of the liver.

The second held a pair of bloodstained, lime-coated combinations — a type of women's underwear with both sleeves and legs. In the third was brown human hair wound up in a Hinde's curler, the ragged handkerchief and the camisole. The fourth and fifth jars held pieces of the bloodstained flannelette pyjama jacket, its brown and green stripes caked with lime. Willcox got to work the next day and, at his request, two days later Marshall brought more samples: a second curler with some hair, part of the intestines, and a large part of the liver. Marshall went back to the remains in the mortuary on 14 August and again selected samples for Willcox: the lungs, more of the intestines, some specimens of muscle, and a third Hinde's curler; another jar held some soil and lime taken from the coffin. Finally he handed over a sample of carbolic powder, which, unbidden, Robinson had sprinkled over the remains in order to keep the smell at bay.

This was not the first time that the evidence had been open to contamination. During the excavation of the grave, according to Dew, the smell got so bad that they had to stop digging while Detective Constable Pitts went out to buy some disinfectant fluid, which he diluted and 'poured around the sides of the excavation in the cellar… none was actually poured on the remains' (MEPO 3/198). A month later Willcox recognized the potential problem, so Pitts was sent to retrieve the first bottle and buy another for comparison. Although Pitts's formal report states that none could have got on the remains in the grave, he told Willcox that it might have, and in fact it had (see Willcox's report of 2 September 1910 in DPP 1/13).

Another potential contamination occurred when between 18 and 22 July the remains were left on a slab in an unlocked room at the Islington mortuary, covered over by stiff white paper from the borough council's storeroom. There was no way to test this paper for possible contaminants because, even though Robinson noted its use in the testimony he gave at the police court on 8 September, he had since used the last of it to wrap up his children's lunches. At the adjourned inquest on 12 September Arthur Newton asked if Robinson appreciated the importance of the paper, to which he replied: 'I never thought any more about that than flying. White paper is healthier than printed paper for lunches'—a declaration which was met by hoots of laughter (*The Times*, 13 September 1910). In later years entire cases would be thrown out of court for such gross forensic blunders, but in 1910 little was thought of such issues and Crippen's defence never queried the matter.

On 23 July Willcox began the toxicological analysis by testing the stomach, kidney and part of the liver for mineral and organic poisons; the arsenic and carbolic acid he found were clearly the result of contamination from the carbolic powder and disinfectant fluid used by the police. Then he began looking for alkaloids, the organic substances to which many medicinal drugs owe their properties. Found in plants, many are highly poisonous and even in minute doses produce characteristic physiological effects. Extracting them is a patient process, and it took Willcox a fortnight. Weighed portions of the stomach, intestines, kidney and liver were subjected to a variety of chemical tests, all of which indicated the presence of an alkaloid. Tests for the common alkaloids (including strychnine, morphine and cocaine) were negative.

On 13 August Pepper watched as Willcox performed a physiological test with extracts from the liver and stomach: he let a drop of the solution fall into the eyes of two cats, which immediately dilated, proving that the alkaloid was of vegetable origin. The cats' pupils were completely paralysed, remaining open even when exposed to a very bright light; the effect lasted up to three days and was also caused by extracts of the kidney and intestine. Willcox's son tells us in his biography of his father that at least one of these cats survived its ordeal and was subsequently named Crippen.

The next step was to find out which alkaloid he was dealing with. Willcox carried out what is known as Vitali's test, treating a few drops of the extracted solution with nitric acid and caustic potash. It immediately turned violet, indicating that the alkaloid was one of those from the deadly nightshade, or henbane plant: atropine, hyoscyamine or hyoscine. The main distinguishing feature is their form: pure hyoscine is a gummy substance, but atropine and hyoscyamine are crystalline. This substance was gummy. When treated with bromine, atropine and hyoscyamine give small brown crystals but hyoscine gives small brown spheres; using this test, Willcox got spheres. He then noted that the alkaloids produced by bacteria during putrefaction (known as animal alkaloids) had never in his experience produced the violet colour or a mydriatic reaction—the dilation of the pupils—on cats' eyes. By 20 August he felt certain that he had found hyoscine in the torso from the cellar.

Lastly, Willcox calculated that the total amount of poison recovered from the internal organs was two-sevenths of a grain (18.5 mg), which corresponded to a total body load of half a grain (32.5 mg). Here, then, was the cause of death: a quarter to half a grain was known to be a fatal dose. He assumed that it had been given as the hydrobromide salt, the form in which it was sold in England; when it was prescribed, which was not often, it was used as a sedative in cases of mania and delirium. The official dose was one-hundredth to five two-hundredths of a grain:

> Hyoscine hydrobromide (or other salt of hyoscine) is a very powerful narcotic poison and in large doses it would produce at first some delirium and stupor, with dryness of the throat and paralysis of the pupils. Very soon complete unconsciousness and coma with paralysis would follow and in a short time (a few hours) death would result. The relatively large amounts of the poison found in the stomach and intestine show that the poison was taken by the mouth. The amounts present in the liver and kidney show that the deceased probably lived some little time (an hour or more) before death occurred. (DPP 1/13)

This marked the culmination of a truly groundbreaking episode in forensic science: a search of the literature revealed the case to be the first in which hyoscine was used to commit a murder. Given its exceptional rarity, Luff (an expert on animal alkaloids) was asked to repeat the experiments and fully confirmed Willcox's results and the conclusions drawn from them. He was ready to counter as absolutely untenable any claim that an animal alkaloid produced by decomposition could have been mistaken for hyoscine (DPP 1/13).

The coup de grâce, the link between the missing Crippen and the poisoned remains in his cellar, was provided by a pharmacist and his assistant (see plate 16). In January 1910, Charles Hetherington recalled, Crippen had called at the New Oxford Street chemists Lewis and Burrows to order five grains of hyoscine hydrobromide on behalf of Munyon's, for 'homeopathic preparations' — such a large amount that they had to get it from the wholesaler. Two days later, on 19 January, Crippen returned to collect his order and sign the poison register.

Although Crippen had purchased many drugs, including morphine and cocaine, from Lewis and Burrows over the past three years, this was the only time he bought hyoscine crystals. It did not take long for the police to realize that Munyon's never used hyoscine: their drugs were made in America and shipped to England ready for sale. Nor did it seem to have a legitimate use in homeopathy. The case against Crippen looked very strong indeed. Now all they had to do was find him.

CHAPTER THREE

An International Manhunt

Once human remains were found in the cellar at 39 Hilldrop Crescent the search for Dr Crippen and Ethel Le Neve commenced in earnest: the police kept a close watch on ports and stations throughout the country and issued bulletins to capitals around the world. Dew assumed that Crippen, being a foreigner, would flee abroad (passports and visas were rarely required for international travel and the couple had in fact left the country), and William Long's revelation about the boy's clothing he had bought suggested how Ethel might be disguised (see plate 13). Further descriptions of the pair were issued on 16 July, and on the same day a full-scale 'Wanted' poster was printed (see p. 4 and plate 12).

Oddly enough, the poster did not mention that Le Neve was likely to be dressed as a boy, nor that she too had false teeth: in an episode that hints at her strength of character, she had had 21 teeth extracted in one sitting by Dr Rylance, convinced they were the cause of the neuralgia she had suffered for years. This poster was translated (the National Archives also holds a copy of the French version) and distributed around the world, while as information continued to pour in, later bulletins and press reports corrected the error about her teeth and added to the physical descriptions: Le Neve tended to walk slowly, while Crippen displayed his teeth prominently when he talked.

On the same day that the poster was printed, Dew appeared at Bow Street police court to apply for a warrant against Crippen and Le Neve:

> for having on or about the 2nd day of February 1910, at 39 Hill-drop Crescent, Camden Road, in the said County and District, wilfully murdered one Cora Crippen, otherwise Belle Elmore, supposed to be the wife of Hawley Harvey Crippen and that they did mutilate and bury some of the remains in the coal cellar at the above address. (DPP 1/13)

The warrant was duly issued by the court's chief magistrate, Sir Albert de Rutzen, and Dew embarked on a frustrating week of false sightings and confusing witness statements; reading and sorting the reports flowing in meant long hours in the office. Several innocent people were arrested on suspicion, including one man who was brought to Scotland Yard twice because he resembled Crippen. On 20 July Dew asked that all post addressed to William Long or Ethel Le Neve's parents and sister be opened and sent to the police, in case the fugitives tried to contact them. The day before, the Home Secretary had authorized a reward of £250 for information leading to their arrest. The public clamour grew, but the seeds that led at last to a real break in the case had already been planted.

On 14 July two detectives from the Blackwall district of London spoke with an (unnamed) officer of the Canadian Pacific Railway Company (CPRC) steamer *Montrose* before she left Millwall dock, bound for Canada via Antwerp. Sergeants Francis Barclay and Thomas Arle gave the officer a full description of Crippen and Le Neve on the chance that they might join the ship at Antwerp, Crippen posing as a clergyman and Ethel as a boy. In his report of 3 August (MEPO 3/198), written no doubt with a view to securing as much credit for himself as possible, Barclay said he suspected the wanted pair might choose the *Montrose* because she was the sort of vessel that could escape close scrutiny. A single-screw steamship of 5,000 tons which travelled at 13 knots per hour, she usually transported cattle and other cargo and carried mostly third-class passengers. Despite these modest functions, however, she was equipped with the latest wireless technology.

Barclay must have been one of those police officers whose hunches always paid off, for it was from the *Montrose* that the thrilling news came: Crippen and Le Neve had been found!

TRANSATLANTIC CHASE

The *Montrose* sailed from Millwall to Antwerp on the evening of 14 July. She was captained by Henry George Kendall, a lieutenant in the Royal Navy reserves who had worked for the CPRC for eight years, two and a half of them as a ship's commander. On the day before she sailed Kendall saw the full written description of Crippen and Le Neve (it is doubtful he was the officer Barclay spoke to), noting that Le Neve might be dressed as a boy. He bought a copy of the international edition of the *Daily Mail* in Antwerp, which had printed the descriptions and photographs of the fugitives, so he was as well informed as everyone else about their appearance.

The *Montrose* embarked for Montreal on the morning of 20 July, carrying 107 crew and 266 passengers, most of them third class. Within three hours Kendall's attention was drawn to two passengers in particular: 'When I saw the boy squeeze the man's hand I thought it strange and unnatural, and it occurred to me at once that they might be Crippen and Le Neve' (Kendall quotes from statement in MEPO 3/198). They passed themselves off as a father and son from Detroit, John Philo Robinson, 55, and 16-year-old John George Robinson, but they were betrayed by their behaviour together and the fit of Master Robinson's trousers, which had split down the back and were held in place with safety pins. Mr Robinson did not have a moustache (Crippen was growing a beard) or wear glasses, but the observant captain noticed that he had a mark on the bridge of his nose; he also noted that Mr Robinson could speak French.

Kendall's police statement, dated 4 August, describes how he kept the pair under observation for two days before speaking to Crippen about sea sickness; the reply he received convinced him he was speaking to a medical man. On the afternoon of 22 July he told his Marconi operator to send a message to England:

> Have strong suspicion that Crippen London Cellar Murderer and accomplice are amongst saloon passengers. Moustache shaved off, growing beard. Accomplice dressed as boy, voice, manner and build undoubtedly a girl.

Mr A. Piers, the shipping manager of the CPRC at Liverpool, got the message (then sometimes called a marconigram) and passed it to the local police, who relayed it to London. Dew received it with jubilation. Here was another event unique in history: the first time that wireless telegraphy was used to track a murderer. On board, Crippen heard the wireless crackle, but had no idea that it was chattering about him. The rest of the world knew what he did not: there could be no escape.

Subsequent police enquiries established that Crippen and Le Neve had travelled from Harwich to Rotterdam on 9 July, arriving there on the morning of the 10th. It was there that, according to Le Neve in *Her Life Story*, she had her hair cut properly: Crippen had chopped it off roughly in Albion House, and a Dutch barber repaired the damage. That evening they departed for Brussels, where they spent the next ten days at the Hotel des Ardennes under the name of Robinson.

Le Neve described this period as a happy one, and said they made no attempt to hide but explored the city thoroughly. The hotel manager remembered things somewhat differently. During their stay the pair kept mostly to their room, leaving only for about two hours each day. The younger of the two spoke in whispers, Robinson senior explaining that his son was deaf and suffering from a throat problem. They had only one tiny piece of luggage between them.

On 13 July, as Dew was preparing to excavate his cellar, Crippen called at the offices of the Red Star Line in Brussels to enquire about passages to Canada. Two days later he bought two tickets to Montreal, paying £21 for a four-berth second-class cabin. The clerk who supervised the boarding (one Schnepp) remembered them, and seems to have been one of the few people who was fooled by Le Neve's disguise — he thought she really was a boy. He also noticed that Crippen had facial eczema, something never mentioned in any other report. Perhaps it was a sign of stress.

While police officers stationed on the Continent were enquiring about their quarry's movements, Dew made preparations to follow them to Canada: the chase was on. Passage was booked for him on the White Star liner *Laurentic*, a faster ship than the *Montrose*, and he sailed from Liverpool on the evening of 23 July under the name of Dewhurst, a nom de plume selected for him by the Liverpool officer who booked the ticket. It was all kept secret (he was met at the station by an officer wearing a red rose in his lapel) to avoid the attentions of journalists. But the news quickly leaked out, and Dew began a battle of wills with the 'gentlemen of the press' that was to last for months.

The longer the hunt for Crippen and Le Neve went on, the

more the press and public began to question the police investigation, especially Dew's role in it. On 26 July the Home Secretary, Winston Churchill, was informed that William Thorne MP intended to raise the subject in Parliament, giving voice to a question that many had been asking: Was Dew guilty of a grave dereliction of duty in not having Crippen followed and his house watched as soon as he came under suspicion? Home Office files show that senior officials debated what answer to give (HO 144/1718/195492). Churchill's view—that he would not discuss the issue while Dew was abroad—won the day. Opinion was otherwise equally divided between those who, like the Police Commissioner Sir Edward Henry, thought the less said the better, and those who wanted to make a much stiffer rebuttal, recognizing that if Crippen had not fled, the crime might never have been discovered.

There were two sides to this argument: there was no evidence of murder when Dew visited Hilldrop Crescent on 8 July, but the fact that Belle Elmore had allegedly sailed for America in the middle of winter without any of her clothes or furs should have triggered an alarm. For the moment, however, the priority had to be the investigation (led during Dew's absence by Superintendent Froest) and preparations for the inquest, committal proceedings and criminal trial that would inevitably follow.

Mid-Atlantic, Dew had another problem to worry about. He expected to reach Quebec on 30 July, about a day ahead of the

Montrose, but he had no idea where the other ship actually was and desperately needed to make contact with Kendall. He spent hours in the *Laurentic*'s wireless room while fruitless attempts were made, but the *Laurentic* was unable to contact the *Montrose* until they were about a day away from Father Point, a lonely little place in the Gulf of St Lawrence where ships stopped to pick up river pilots. Dew had obtained permission from the Quebec police to land there, which was not usually allowed because of quarantine regulations. It was to become the scene of his most famous encounter.

In a letter written to his superiors from Quebec on 2 August (all quotes from MEPO 3/198) Dew was careful to inform them that, regardless of what had been claimed in press reports, his identity was not discovered until the day before he landed at Father Point; reporters from the *Daily Mail* and the *Montreal Star* got the scoop. He arrived at 3 pm on Friday 30 July to find about thirty reporters and cameramen waiting. He was 'absolutely mobbed' by members of the press, 'cameras were thrust in my face and I was practically at their mercy', but he refused to talk to them or to answer any of the numerous wireless messages that were sent to the *Laurentic* for him.

Dew settled down to wait for the *Montrose*. He was met by Chief Inspector McCarthy and Inspector Denis of the Quebec Provincial Police (neither of whom could speak much English), and the next day sent a message asking Kendall to keep Crippen and Le Neve under discreet observation, to prevent any attempt at suicide. Kendall remained convinced that the fugitives had no idea their identities had been discovered.

The *Montrose* reached Father Point at about 8 am on Sunday 1 August, and Dew hatched a plot to board in disguise. Kendall had told him that Crippen was on deck and Dew feared that if he saw him coming, he might jump overboard: 'I procured the loan of a pilot's uniform, and this made a really good disguise.' Weeks later, one of the ship's officers described the scene:

> Crippen was walking up and down the deck with the ship's
> doctor when he saw the pilot boat coming. There were more
> than the usual number in it because of the police who were
> there. Crippen looked at the boat and said to the doctor, 'There
> are a lot of pilots today, aren't there?' The doctor made no reply,
> and then Chief Constable McCarthy of the Canadian police
> stepped aboard, and then Inspector Dew, and they collared
> him. (*Morning Advertiser*, 20 August 1910)

In fact, once the policemen had boarded Dew went to Kendall's cabin while the Canadian officers fetched Mr Robinson. Crippen must surely have felt a thrill of fear at their approach. As he came face to face with Dew they recognized each other almost immediately, and Crippen made no attempt to dispute his identity. When the charge of murder and mutilation was read out, he said nothing. Still fearing a suicidal leap, McCarthy handcuffed him, but Crippen replied: 'I won't. I am more than satisfied because the anxiety has been too awful.'

Dew then went to Crippen's cabin, where he found Le Neve

'reclining on a couch', wearing the brown suit that William Long had bought. In his view, it was 'difficult to believe that any person with an average amount of intelligence could ever have believed her to be a boy'. She too remained silent when the arrest warrant was read, but later said that she had not seen any English papers since she left London and that if she had, she would have contacted someone. As the enormity of her situation began to sink in, she collapsed. Dew arranged for the ship's steward to get her some women's clothing, and tried to make her as comfortable as circumstances would allow.

When Dew returned to search Crippen, he asked after Le Neve. Dew replied that she was 'agitated, but I am doing all I can for her'. 'It's only fair to say that she knows nothing about it. I never told her anything,' Crippen replied. Later the prosecution was to ask the jury to consider what 'it' was that he did not tell her, if not a murder?

The search revealed that Crippen had sewn four diamond rings, the rising sun brooch and a paste butterfly brooch to his vest; he had $10 in cash, Le Neve had $60. He also had two notes, written on the back of Mr Robinson's business cards. (No one ever tried to find out where these cards came from, but he must have had them printed in Antwerp; there are transcriptions in CRIM 1/117.) One intended apparently for Ethel read:

> I cannot stand the horrors I go through every night any longer
> and as I see nothing bright ahead and money has come to an
> end I have made up my mind to jump overboard tonight. I

know I have spoilt your life but I hope some day you can learn
to forgive me. With last words of love, Your H.

The other was apparently part of an escape plan: 'Shall we
wait until tonight about 10 or 11 o'clock?' At his trial Crippen
claimed that one of the ship's four quartermasters had offered
to help him escape by faking a suicidal jump overboard and
that these cards were part of the scheme, but he was unable to
name the quartermaster concerned. The prosecution stressed
the fact that a man suffering from 'horrors' must have a guilty
conscience.

Dew could only hold the crowd of reporters at bay for an
hour after the arrests, and since every one of them had bought
a ticket to sail on the *Montrose* from Father Point to Montreal,
the ship swarmed with them. Some went to astonishing lengths
to get a glimpse of the prisoners, but none succeeded. Stories
that gave details of the arrests were entirely false, as were the
numerous reports that Crippen had confessed and the claim
that Dew had expressed his belief in Le Neve's innocence:
'When newspapers go to this length, it is difficult to know what
lies they will resort to.'

Dew was offered 'fabulous sums' if he would give an interview or allow photos to be taken of his prisoners—journalists
were especially keen to get a picture of Le Neve in boy's
clothing. In the absence of hard facts they made their stories
up, but pursued Dew everywhere while he was in Canada. His
plaintive grumble, 'my life has been made a perfect burden',

was followed up by a reminder of his steadfastness in the face of adversity: 'Every possible ruse has been adopted to break through the reserve I have maintained from the first.' The American reporters, who were accustomed to police cooperation, were the worst offenders, and Dew took a perverse pleasure in the fact that his secrecy and civility annoyed them: 'Justice does not seem to weigh with these people, so long as they get copy.'

CAPTURED

When they landed at Quebec City on 1 August, Crippen was taken to the city jail while McCarthy took Le Neve to his own home to be looked after by his wife and daughter, before she was transferred to the prison infirmary. Crippen spent his time reading (including, to the great delight of the pressmen outside, a murder novel by Edgar Wallace); his lover was fitted for new clothes, paid for out of the money the police had confiscated.

Plans were immediately made to bring the couple back to London. On 4 August Sergeant Mitchell, accompanied by two female warders from Holloway prison (there were no suitable female police officers) embarked on the *Lake Manitoba* for Canada. Mitchell carried extradition papers; the wardresses, Sarah Maria Stone and Julia Foster, were to watch over Le Neve on the voyage home. By the time they arrived on 14 August the papers were unnecessary: the prisoners had agreed to waive extradition (innocent people had nothing to fear) and were eager to return home.

On 2 August a London newspaper offered Crippen £500 for his life story, and he received a telegram from Arthur Newton in which the well-known solicitor informed him of his intention to defend him at the request of friends. If a friend really was involved (Newton was not above lying and may have been acting for a newspaper, or simply seizing the initiative in a case that promised unprecedented publicity), Julie Early in *Victorian Studies* suggests that it was Scott Hamilton, who paid him a £100 retainer. At his trial Crippen could not or would not say who the friend was.

Newton, who was two years older than his new client, was described by those who knew him as an extremely astute and resourceful solicitor with a wide experience of criminal cases. In 1907 he had famously secured the acquittal of Robert Wood in the case of the Camden Town murder of a prostitute, working with the barrister Edward Marshall Hall. From one Camden Town killing to another: Crippen accepted the offer with alacrity, and was advised in a letter of 3 August 1910 'not to say a single syllable' about the case (DPP 1/13). Ethel Le Neve's father and sister each hired a lawyer for her, but by mid-September she too was instructing Newton.

At Dew's suggestion, first-class passage home was booked for the party of six on the White Star liner *Megantic*, sister ship of the *Laurentic*. She embarked for Liverpool on 20 August, the same day that Willcox discovered hyoscine in the cellar remains. Unaware that the scientific evidence against him had grown even stronger, Crippen seemed in good spirits throughout the voyage, though he was clearly concerned about Le Neve. Dew spent a great deal of time with him, and found him a 'remarkable little man'; he did his best to ensure the comfort of both prisoners, but kept them apart from one another. Although he later claimed in his memoirs that he allowed them one swift reunion on board the *Megantic*, this was fiction; Nicholas Connell in his biography of Dew has pointed out that if this episode occurred, it was on the train between Liverpool and London. In any case, both later expressed their gratitude for the courtesy shown them.

Although they had sailed under aliases (Crippen was Cyrus Field), when the *Megantic* docked at Liverpool on Saturday 27 August she was met by a huge crowd that made its anti-Crippen feelings known. For the first time he showed signs of nerves, so Dew gave him his overcoat, which was so big on him that it came down to his ankles (see plate 17). With the collar turned up and his hat pulled down low, as a photo of Dew and Crippen coming down the gangplank shows, his features were well hidden.

Crippen and Le Neve were immediately taken to London by train, where they were greeted by an even more hostile crowd outside Bow Street police station. They spent Saturday night and Sunday in the cells, and on the morning of Monday 29 August they were brought briefly into court so that the prosecution could seek an adjournment for eight days. It was made clear that the charge against Le Neve would be reduced to being an accessory after a murder.

The Times reported on 30 August that Crippen entered the court first, but on reaching the dock he stood aside to allow Le Neve to pass. By then he was again clean shaven except for his moustache, and he was dressed in a light grey suit; the long frock coat had large lapels of grey silk (see plate 18). Le Neve wore a navy blue coat and skirt, with a large blue hat and thick blue veil that effectively shrouded her face from curious onlookers. She smiled only once, when Dew mentioned that on being arrested she was wearing a boy's suit.

Both were formally remanded into custody: Crippen was sent to Brixton prison while Le Neve went to Holloway. Staff at Brixton had some anxious moments in advance of Crippen's arrival, and decided to keep him under constant supervision to prevent suicide and leaks to the press. This required additional manpower, and the Prison Commissioners agreed reluctantly, fearing that instituting new procedures simply because an alleged murderer was infamous was rather extravagant and might set an unwelcome precedent (PCOM 8/30).

The proceedings at Bow Street (which was used because its jurisdiction extended to all areas of London) occupied four days, 6, 8, 14 and 21 September, and terminated in the committal of both prisoners for trial at the Old Bailey. Crippen said only that he was not guilty; he called no witnesses. On none of the occasions when he might have given an explanation for his flight did he do so: on arrest, when the warrant was read, when charged with murder, and when committed for trial.

The inquest on the remains found at Hilldrop Crescent ran largely in parallel. Opened and adjourned on 18 July, it resumed on 15 August, continuing on 12, 19 and 26 September. The remains were found to be 'parts of the body of Cora Crippen alias Belle Elmore', and a verdict of wilful murder was brought against her husband (CRIM 1/117).

In September Newton auctioned off Crippen's furniture to pay the rent on Hilldrop Crescent (which thereafter became the police's problem), and on the 28th staff at Brixton discovered that he was planning to sell Crippen's life story to raise money for the defence; it had been taken down in shorthand during the various meetings they held. Reputable solicitors understood that interviews should be concerned solely with the case, but the maverick Newton knew that no rule forbade other types of discussion; in fact he had done this sort of thing before. Churchill himself dealt with the problem:

> It is impossible to aggravate the publicity and sensationalism which has surrounded this case. We must not fetter the accused on grounds of taste... Now that permission has been asked formally for the publication on grounds that the money is needed for purposes of the prisoner's defence, the application will be granted. (PCOM 8/30)

The trial date was set for Tuesday 18 October.

The Anglo-American Telegraph Company, LTD.

ESTABLISHED 1866

FOUR CABLES TO AMERICA
(AUTOMATIC DUPLEX SYSTEM)

IN DIRECT TELEGRAPHIC COMMUNICATION WITH

NEW YORK	CHICAGO	MONTREAL	ST LOUIS	CENTRAL and	NEW ZEALAND
BALTIMORE	CINCINNATI	PHILADELPHIA	SAN FRANCISCO	SOUTH AMERICA	TASMANIA
BOSTON	GALVESTON	NEWFOUNDLAND	WEST INDIES	AUSTRALIA	&c &c

OFFICE STAMP & DATE

Time Rec⁴ 4 8ʰ m. from *Wireless*   N° Words 22

Place *Smeeth.*

Quebec

"Via // ANGLO."

Handcuffs

TO {

London England

Confirming Former Cable

Arrest made arrive

Quebec midnight Sunday

Suggest matron and

Metchell Crippen threatened

Suicide Writing soon

Dew

PLEASE HAND YOUR REPLY DIRECT TO THIS OFFICE.   ONLY DIRECT ROUTE TO NEWFOUNDLAND.   P.T.O.

15 Telegram sent by Chief Inspector Walter Dew from Canada,
confirming the arrest of Crippen and le Neve, 1 August 1910.
(MEPO 3/198)

SUBJECT Murder

Poisons traced

to H.H.Crippen

REFERENCE TO PAPERS.

15418.

METROPOLITAN POLICE.

CRIMINAL INVESTIGATION DEPARTMENT,

NEW SCOTLAND YARD,

REGISTRY
RECEIVED
3 AUG 1910
C.I.D.

2nd day of August 1910.

I beg to report having, as directed, made

enquiries at Messrs Lewis & Burrows, Chemists, 108

New Oxford Street, with a view to ascertain if

any poisons had been sold to Dr. H.H.Crippen, this

year.

Upon making the enquiry, I found that Dr.

Crippen was a customer to the firm, and well

known to the manager, and assistants, at the shop

and that he had on 19th January last, purchased

5 grains of hyoscine hydrobromate. He said he

wanted it for homoeopathic preparations for

Munyon's, and signed the poisons book for it, in

name of H.H.Crippen.

About 15th or 16th June last, Dr. Crippen

handed in a written order for 2 grains of

perchloride of mercury. This order was signed

H.H.Crippen. The Doctor was served with it, and

the order is still in the possession of Messrs

Lewis & Burrows.

Statement of Mr Harold Kirby, Asistant to

Messrs Lewis & Burrows, who actually supplied

Dr. Crippen with the poisons, attached.

B

16 *Left*: Police report on the discovery that hyoscine was sold to Dr Crippen at Lewis & Burrows on 19 January 1910. (MEPO 3/198)

17 *Above*: The party disembarking at Liverpool on 27 August 1910; Crippen is escorted by Dew, and wearing his coat.

18 *Above*: Crippen and le Neve in the dock at Bow Street magistrates' court.

19 *Top right*: Request from the Medical Officer of Health for burial of the remains of Cora Crippen, 7 October 1910. The general assumption that the remains were Cora's, rather than a stranger's, may have been prejudicial to Crippen's case. (MEPO 3/198)

20 *Below right*: The frenzied scene outside the Old Bailey during Crippen's trial.

W.J.W.

PUBLIC HEALTH DEPARTMENT.

ALFRED EDWIN HARRIS.
MEDICAL OFFICER OF HEALTH.

TOWN HALL,
UPPER STREET,
ISLINGTON, N.

7th October 1910.

Sir,

Now that the inquest on the remains of Mrs Crippen is closed, it is most desirable that owing to their state of decomposition they should be buried as soon as possible. They are in the Mortuary here, and are likely to cause a serious nuisance.

Under these circumstances I would be glad to learn that steps have been taken for their interment.

I am,

Yours obediently.

Medical Officer of Health.

21 *Above*: Dr Crippen in the dock at the Old Bailey.

22 *Left*: Richard Muir, who conducted the prosecution case against Crippen.

23 *Below*: Crippen's notice of appeal against his conviction, 26 October 1910. (HO 144/1718/195492)

FORM XXXIV.
597   195492
CRIMINAL APPEAL ACT, 1907.

NOTICE OF APPEAL OR APPLICATION FOR LEAVE TO APPEAL AGAINST CONVICTION OR SENTENCE.

To the REGISTRAR OF THE COURT OF CRIMINAL APPEAL.

Name of Appellant *Hawley Harvey Crippen*
Convicted at the*   C.C.C.   held at *Old Bailey*
Offence of which convicted*   *Wilful Murder*
Sentence   *Death*
Date when convicted   *22nd. 10. 10.*
Date when sentence passed   *22 - 10 - 10*
Name of Prison*   *Pentonville*

I the above-named Appellant hereby give you notice that I desire to appeal to the Court of Criminal Appeal against my conviction*

on the grounds hereinafter set forth on page 2 of this notice.

(Signed)* *Hawley Harvey Crippen*
Appellant.
Dated this *26th* day of *October* A.D. 1910.

The Appellant must answer the following questions:

QUESTION.   ANSWER.

1. Did the Judge before whom you were tried grant you a Certificate that it was a fit case for Appeal?   *No*

2. Do you desire the Court of Criminal Appeal to assign you legal aid?   *No*
   If your answer to this question is "Yes," then answer the following questions:—
   (a) What was your occupation and what wages, salary or income were you receiving before your conviction?
   (b) Have you any means to enable you to obtain legal aid for yourself?   *Yes*
   (c) Is any Solicitor now acting for you? If so, give his name and address.   *Mr Arthur Newton 23 Great Marlborough Street. W.*

3. Do you desire to be present when the Court considers your case?   *Yes*

4. Do you desire to apply for leave to call any witnesses on your appeal?   *No.*
   If your answer to this question is "Yes," you must obtain form XXVI, fill it up, and forward it with this notice.

[TURN OVER.

2
Grounds of Appeal or Application.

(1) That one of the Jurymen after I had been given in charge of the Jury absented himself from the rest of the Jury without either he or the rest of the Jury being given in charge of the proper officer of the [Court]

[That] the identity of the remains found at Hilldrop Crescent was not established

[That] the Judge did not sufficiently place [before] the Jury the question of there being no [mark] upon the piece of skin measuring [six in]ches by six inches.

[That] the Judge misdirected the Jury in [telling] them that the onus of proof, that [a mark] upon the piece of skin, measuring [six inch]es by six inches, was not a scar [was upon] me.

[Please] be supplied free of charge with a [copy of the no]te of the proceedings at the [trial and forwar]ded to my Solicitor Mr Arthur Newton [Great Marl]borough Street, Regent Street, London W.

Harvey Crippen

Pinkerton's National Detective Agency;

FOUNDED BY ALLAN PINKERTON 1850.

WM. A. PINKERTON, CHICAGO. } PRINCIPALS
ALLAN PINKERTON, NEW YORK. }

GEO. D. BANGS. GENERAL MANAGER NEW YORK.

NEW YORK
BOSTON
MONTREAL
TORONTO
BUFFALO

PHILADELPHIA
BALTIMORE
PITTSBURGH
CLEVELAND

OFFICES.
CHICAGO
CINCINNATI
DETROIT
ST. LOUIS
ST. PAUL

DENVER
KANSAS CITY
NEW ORLEANS
SALT LAKE CITY

SAN FRANCISCO
SEATTLE
SPOKANE
PORTLAND, ORE.
LOS ANGELES

#C.O.15418/802.

New York, December 27, 1910.

Assistant Commissioner of Police,
Criminal Investigation Department,
New Scotland Yard, London S.W.

Dear Sir:-

We are in receipt of copy of your letter of December
19th to our Chicago office in re H.H.Crippen, and as per your
request we take pleasure in forwarding you today original receipt
from Bruce Miller for $450.00 advance given him when he left New York,
also agreement made with Mrs. Hunn, under which she was paid $100.00
at the time she sailed, to which her signature is affixed, and which
takes the place of a receipt. This latter agreement, as you
will note, is addressed to Supt. Froest and was to be delivered
by Mrs. Hunn personally, which, however, she failed to do through
an oversight.

We also enclose receipt from the Hamburg-American Line S.S.Co.
for the passages of Bruce Miller and Mrs. Hunn. Receipts obtained from these people at the time of our final
settlement with them, were forwarded to Supt. Froest under date of
November 7th, but as it is possible that these receipts were
mislaid we enclose you copies of same, as these receipts were
obtained by us in triplicate.

Yours truly,
PINKERTON'S NATIONAL DETECTIVE AGENCY,
by [signature]

H.M. Prison,
Pentonville,
21. 8. 11.

9146 H.H. Crippen.

Inventory of Clothing, etc.

1 Overcoat
1 Coat
1 Waistcoat
1 Trousers
2 Hats
4 Shirts
1 Pr. Drawers
4 Socks
5 Handkerchiefs
1   Do.   Silk
10 Collars
2 Bows
1 Pr. Gloves
6 Books
1 Gladstone bag
1 Toothbrush
        s   d
Cash 5/4½
1 Pair of Spectacles

(sgd) W. Middleton Warder.

To the Governor.

24 *Above*: Letter from Allan
Pinkerton to Scotland Yard, 27
December 1910, referring to the
costs of bringing Theresa Hunn
and Bruce Miller to London.
(MEPO 3/198)

25 *Left*: The prison inventory
of Crippen's possessions to be
returned to Ethel le Neve,
21 August 1911. (PCOM 8/30)

CHAPTER FOUR

The Law Takes its Course

In the decades before the First World War, responsibility for prosecuting criminal offences lay largely with the police and private citizens, but the Director of Public Prosecutions (a post created in 1879) took on an increasing proportion of the most serious cases following the formation of a new Department of Public Prosecutions in 1908. In 1910 its director was Sir Charles Mathews, who was keen to indict Crippen as soon as he returned to England. Mathews assigned the case to the two Treasury Counsel (barristers who prosecuted for the Crown at the Central Criminal Court, usually known as the Old Bailey), Richard Muir and his junior Travers Humphreys.

It was customary for one of the two Law Officers—the Attorney-General or Solicitor-General—to lead for the Crown in important capital cases, especially if poison was involved. The fact that the prosecution of Crippen and Le Neve was entrusted to Muir and Humphreys suggests that the case was not seen as particularly complex. It had a high public profile but, as Humphreys put it in his memoir *Criminal Days*, 'the only possible defence was the old plea: you cannot convict me as nobody saw me do it'.

Muir (see plate 22), a Scot by birth, had a fearsome reputation for building impregnable cases around cold, hard facts. He was regarded by his admirers as logical and fair, by his critics as ponderous and relentless. His biographer Sidney Felstead recalled that when Crippen heard Muir was to conduct the prosecution against him, he told Arthur Newton: 'It is most unfortunate that he is against me. I wish it had been anybody else but him. I fear the worst.' He was right to do so. Muir (Dickie, to his friends) worked long hours for weeks to construct a watertight case, and insisted that everyone else do the same. His trial papers, now in the National Archives, reveal his strategy: dangerous points were underlined in red pencil, while other colours were used to indicate the material on which to examine, cross-examine and re-examine witnesses.

It was at Muir's insistence that Bruce Miller, whom Crippen had alleged his wife had run off to join, was found. By late summer police enquiries had got nowhere, so on 15 September the DPP contacted Pinkerton's Detective Agency to see if they could trace him, find out when he had last seen Belle Elmore or received letters from her, and try to discover information about her operation (MEPO 3/198). Miller, now a successful estate agent, was found in Chicago, and Pinkerton's brokered a deal where he agreed to come to England to testify for what amounted to a fee: $25 per day for a minimum of 30 days, and $5 per day while in England, with first-class fare and return passage from Chicago to London.

Pinkerton's then discovered that Theresa Hunn, Belle's sister, had a clear memory of a scar on the lower part of her abdomen, so arrangements were also made for her to attend the trial at a rate of $10 per day from the time she left her home in New Jersey till she returned, with second-class return fare. She and Miller travelled together on the SS *Deutschland* on 8 October, met Dew at Plymouth on the 14th, testified on the first day of Crippen's trial, and were back in New York by 4 November. Pinkerton's submitted a bill for $1,442.79 (MEPO 3/198; see plate 24).

Both Muir and Humphreys seem to have thought that after Dew's return from Canada he lost interest in the case and failed to give it the attention it deserved. He left Belle's furs in the house, and accepted Jones Brothers' initial response to his enquiry about the pyjamas found with the remains, which was that it was impossible to say when they had been sold. Humphreys wrote in his memoirs, 'It was on the very eve of the trial that Muir determined to make a last effort to obtain information which he felt sure must be in existence.' It was. A questionnaire sent to the company's employees led to new information about a specific purchase.

Muir and Humphreys decided that Crippen and Le Neve should be tried separately; this is conveyed in a memo from Assistant DPP Guy Stephenson to Mathews on 6 October (all quotes from DPP 1/13). In order to convict Le Neve of being an accessory, Crippen had to be convicted of murder. If her lawyer proved skilful in cross-examining the prosecution witnesses, it might create enough doubt that just one juror 'might decline to convict Crippen, and a disagreement would of course be disastrous'. Including Le Neve in the case against Crippen would make the key goal of convicting him more difficult to achieve, and that was to be avoided at all costs. In fact, it appears that Muir had no intention that Ethel Le Neve should face a jury at all; Stephenson agreed that 'the result of the proceedings against Le Neve was of very little importance'. But, in the event, two trials were held.

Arthur Newton tried to retain F.E. Smith (later Lord Birkenhead) to defend Crippen, but he declined in favour of the easier task of defending the lady. Next Newton approached Edward Marshall Hall, then the most famous defence barrister in the country, but he refused (various reasons have been suggested; see p. 102), upon which Newton offered the brief to Alfred Tobin, a King's Counsel who later became a judge.

On 11 October 1910 the remains from the cellar at 39 Hilldrop Crescent were buried under the name of Cora Crippen at St Pancras Roman Catholic Cemetery, Finchley. Although Newton had raised no objection, he baulked somewhat at their being buried in her name, and an article published in *The Referee* on 9 October suggested it would be prejudicial to Crippen's case given that his defence was that the remains were those of some stranger. Dew consulted Mathews, who decided that because the coroner had issued a burial order there could be no objection (MEPO 3/198). The funeral went ahead without incident, but it proved an ill omen for the little doctor.

THE TRIAL

The trial of Dr Hawley Harvey Crippen for the murder of his wife opened in No. 1 Court of the new Central Criminal Court building (see plates 20 and 21) on Tuesday 18 October before the Lord Chief Justice of England, Viscount Alverstone. His personality dominated the proceedings, and the sharp questions and comments he put to witnesses show that he thought Crippen was guilty. Muir and Humphreys were joined by S. Ingleby Oddie, a medically qualified barrister who later became the coroner for Westminster. Tobin, who was experienced, intelligent and effective, was assisted by Huntly Jenkins and Henry Roome. They had a difficult task before them.

Huge crowds gathered outside the court, while the few who were lucky enough to have a ticket (an innovation specially designed for the trial of the century) made their way inside to the public gallery. Usually occupied by a few homeless men and prisoners' relatives, the gallery was crowded with theatre folk and well-dressed, mainly female onlookers. Heads turned as one when Crippen entered. Sprucely dressed and looking remarkably well for a man in his position, he went straight to the dock and gazed round the court. He had discarded the grey frock-coat suit he had worn at Bow Street in favour of a black suit in the same style. Asked whether he was guilty or not guilty, he replied in a clear and steady voice: 'Not guilty, my lord.'

The prosecution case was straightforward. Crippen was in love with another woman, and he needed money. In December 1909 his wife gave a year's notice of her intent to withdraw the £600 they had on deposit, on 31 January 1910 his 16-year relationship with Munyon's ended and he lost his weekly salary, and his other businesses were unlikely sources of income. He killed his wife, pawned her jewels for £195 and moved Ethel Le Neve into Hilldrop Crescent. His explanation for Belle Elmore's disappearance—that she had flown into a rage when he failed to show Paul Martinetti to the lavatory and left, perhaps to join Bruce Miller—could be dismissed, the first part being too trivial to require comment, the second untrue in fact. Where, then, was Belle Elmore? Whose remains were found in the cellar? If they were hers, who mutilated her body and buried it there? Who had the opportunity, the skill and the access? How did she die? If she was poisoned, who administered the poison, and where did he or she get it?

The trial lasted five days. Witnesses on the first day included Mrs Martinetti, William Long, Miller (who denied any affair with 'Brown Eyes' and gave little impression that they shared the sort of passion that might have survived a six-year separation), Theresa Hunn and a bank manager who provided information about the Crippens' accounts. Dew went into the witness box on the morning of the second day, and read out Crippen's long statement. In the afternoon Pepper stated his findings in regard to the human remains and the scar. On the following day Spilsbury testified that the mark was a scar from the lower abdomen, Willcox and Luff described how they had found hyoscine, Hetherington proved that Crippen had bought hyoscine hydrobromide, and Adeline Harrison confirmed that Belle Elmore had dyed her hair blonde.

The third day finished with Tobin's opening speech for the defence. How could Crippen have disposed of the body between 1.30 am on 1 February and his arrival at the office the next morning? Why kill his wife 11 months before she could get the money? Crippen had shown no sign of odd behaviour until, fearing arrest on suspicion, he fled. He had only sold what he himself had paid for. Belle had frequently threatened to leave. Crucially, the body in the cellar was not that of Belle Elmore.

Crippen was then examined by Jenkins. There were only three other defence witnesses: Drs Turnbull and Wall, who would have better stayed away, and Dr Alexander Wynter Blyth, a toxicologist brought in to refute Willcox's evidence about hyoscine by claiming that animal alkaloids would give similar test results; he succeeded only in making himself look foolish.

Of course, Crippen had to testify in his own defence; if he had not, the jury would probably have taken it as an admission of guilt. By doing so, however, he subjected himself to Muir's deadly cross-examination and thereby condemned himself as a poor liar who told an impossible story. His admission that he made no effort of any kind to trace his wife after she disappeared told against him, as did the fact that he could not give the names of anyone for whom he had prescribed a homeopathic medicine containing hyoscine.

Then Muir played his trump card: he produced William Chilvers, a buyer for Jones Brothers, after Crippen's own testimony made his evidence material to the case. Crippen claimed that the remains must have been buried before he moved in, and that the odd pair of pyjama trousers found in the house had been purchased in 1905 or 1906 and were unrelated to the jacket in the grave. But Chilvers stated that the fabric was not available until 1908, and that two pairs of pyjamas in the same pattern as the jacket in the grave had been sold to Mrs Crippen on 5 January 1909 (for 17s 9d, cash on delivery). Here was proof that tied Crippen to the body in his cellar. If any doubts remained, Chilvers added that Jones Brothers had not become a limited company until 1906, further tying the remains to Crippen's occupation of the house.

With the spectre of the hangman looming over his client, Tobin then gave his closing speech for the defence. His main points included a detail that Crippen had mentioned in the dock: Ethel Le Neve slept at the house on 2 February, and it was inconceivable that he would have taken her there within a few hours of the alleged murder and disposal of the body. His flight arose from fear that he might be held in prison until his missing, but living, wife was found, and the money could not be touched for months. Lastly, were the remains really those of a woman?

In his closing speech, Muir first pointed out that Crippen was a liar engaged in an illicit affair, and then reiterated the key line of reasoning against him: human remains were found buried in his cellar, wrapped in his pyjamas and containing a fatal dose of a rare poison he admitted buying just days before his wife mysteriously disappeared.

The judge's detailed summing up marshalled the facts of the evidence to provide the jury with guidance as to the weight to attach to it — a relatively new judicial practice which offered far more potential to sway opinion than the traditional habit of simply reading out extracts from the testimony. And Alverstone left listeners in no doubt as to his views on the main issues to consider: the strong medical evidence of identity, how and when the remains got into the house, where was the hyoscine, and why didn't Crippen try to find his wife?

The jury retired to deliberate at 2.15 pm and returned 27 minutes later to deliver their unanimous verdict: guilty. Offered the traditional opportunity to state any reason why he should not be sentenced accordingly, Crippen only protested his innocence. Donning the black cap, the judge reminded him that he had been convicted on evidence that no reasonable man could

doubt. *The Times* reported that the condemned man heard the
verdict and death sentence with an ashen face, and required
medical aid when he was taken from the dock.

Crippen was driven directly from the Old Bailey to Pentonville, where he became prisoner 9146. His belongings recorded
in the property book, he was strip-searched, given prison
clothes and taken to the condemned cell. Although prison
officials were constantly alert to the possibility that he
might attempt suicide, he was to prove a model prisoner who
won their respect and sympathy. The execution date was set
for 8 November.

After the trial all the police officers involved were formally
commended, and Sir Charles Mathews authorized small
rewards: Dew and Mitchell were singled out for particular
credit, receiving £4 and £2 respectively, while the rest got 10s or
15s each. Mathews was also careful to thank his key medical
witnesses, and a copy of his letter to Willcox remains in the
National Archives. In it he offers thanks for the

> advice, instruction, and assistance which you rendered to my
> Counsel outside all official hours, since I am told that, on many
> occasions, you were with them until close upon midnight ... I
> too cordially congratulate you upon the fact that, of the two
> scientific views presented for the consideration of the Jury, it
> was yours which found almost immediate acceptance by them.
> (DPP 1/13)

THE TRIAL OF ETHEL LE NEVE

Four days after her lover was sentenced to death for the murder
of his wife, Ethel Le Neve was tried at the Old Bailey on the
charge of being an accessory after the fact. She faced the same
judge and trio of barristers who had so systematically shredded
Crippen's defence, but Le Neve was in a different position alto-
gether. To establish the charge, the prosecution sought to show
that she knew Crippen was a murderer when she fled with him,
not least because she had worn some of his dead wife's clothes
and jewels, and given others away. Her lawyer—the brilliant
F.E. Smith KC, MP—was, like others who met her at the time,
convinced that she knew nothing of the crime, and would not
allow Muir to shift the burden of proof: merely cutting her hair
and boarding the *Montrose* did not prove she knew she was
fleeing from justice. Spectators, including the Home Secretary,
watched with interest.

The bare facts of the case had already been established, and
the now familiar evidence given by Dew, Pepper, Willcox and
other witnesses was repeated briefly. Muir wasted little time in
turning to the key plank in his argument: Le Neve had suffered
an emotional crisis which appeared to be resolved around the
date when Mrs Crippen disappeared, hinting at knowledge of
the murder. Smith placed the date a week or so earlier, so that it
could have nothing to do with the murder. Everything hinged
on the testimony of Le Neve's former landlady, Emily Jackson.

In her original deposition (DPP 1/13) Mrs Jackson described a night in late January on which Le Neve had returned home in a state of terrible agitation, shaking and unable to eat. The next day she was too ill to go to work. When pressed to share her troubles, she said that it was due to 'the doctor'. Mrs Jackson, whom she called Ma or Mum, assumed she meant she had had another miscarriage, but Le Neve said that the problem was his wife: 'when I see them going away together, it makes me realize my position; what she is, and what I am' (Muir underlined these words heavily in red).

Le Neve went on: 'She has been threatening to go away some time with another man and the doctor will divorce her.' Mrs Jackson advised her to tell Crippen how she felt; she did this the next day, and returned home to report that he had promised to marry her. About a week later, almost certainly 2 February, she told her friend 'Somebody has gone away at last.' She was more cheerful after that, and about a week later she began to sleep at his house one or two nights a week, until finally she moved in with him on 12 March.

Having originally told the police that the incident in question had happened in late January, Mrs Jackson was vaguer under cross-examination. Smith established that Le Neve had been depressed throughout January, at her lowest ebb around the 25th or 26th, and much recovered about a week before Belle Elmore's disappearance. There was thus no reason to suppose that she had suffered the sudden shock of discovering that her lover had murdered his wife. Smith called no witnesses for the defence, and following a brief closing speech for the Crown, he delivered a powerful and eloquent address on behalf of his client. He painted her as a neurotic but gentle girl entirely in the power of an immoral older man: it was easy to imagine that she fled with Crippen to avoid separation from him, impossible to believe that he would ever have told her the truth.

Following a remarkably favourable summing up by Lord Alverstone ('If Crippen had told her, not only might it have been dangerous to himself, but do you not think that it might have changed her feelings towards him?'), the jury took just 20 minutes to find her not guilty. Le Neve immediately left the court with her sister and brother-in-law, and a few days later she sold her story to *Lloyd's Weekly News*.

THE APPEAL

After Crippen's trial ended the judge lost no time in writing to the Home Secretary to express his satisfaction at the verdict. He knew there would undoubtedly be an appeal and so enclosed his notes of the case, but could 'conceive no ground which should prevent the death sentence being carried into effect' (HO 144/1718/195492).

Crippen heard the news of Ethel Le Neve's acquittal with immense relief, and was still hopeful of a positive outcome for himself. His appeal against conviction was filed on 26 October (see plate 23) and heard on 5 November, the same barristers who had acted for the prosecution and defence in the trial appearing again at the Court of Criminal Appeal. Against normal procedure, Crippen was permitted to be present because new evidence was heard. There were three grounds for appeal:

1. On the second day of the trial one of the jurors became separated from the rest.
2. The evidence given by William Chilvers should not have been allowed.
3. The identity of the remains found at 39 Hilldrop Crescent was not established, and the judge misdirected the jury by telling them that it was.

The three appeal judges first acknowledged that if there had been an opportunity to tamper with the juror — who had briefly been absent through illness — they might quash the conviction, but as there was no such evidence the point must be dismissed.

Tobin then submitted that the evidence given by Chilvers was wrongly admitted because it could have been given as part of the case for the prosecution, so should not have been allowed as rebutting evidence. A pyjama jacket had been found on 13 July with the remains, and two suits and an odd pair of trousers on 14 July, but the defence had sought to show in court that the body might have been buried before February 1910. Crippen had said that the odd trousers were part of a set purchased long before, which certainly the Crown could have anticipated.

His final point concerned the sex of the remains and the judge's attitude to them: Lord Alverstone had referred more than once to the body being that of a woman while the issue was still in dispute. The famous scar could easily have been caused by pressure during burial; and Alverstone's remarks about the scar and the navel ('In order to satisfy you that it is not Cora Crippen the defence must have satisfied you that there is no scar there') had wrongly placed the onus of proof on Crippen.

In reply, Muir explained that although Chilvers's statement was taken on 17 October, he received it after the trial had begun, so that Chilvers's formal identification of the remains of the jacket found in the grave occurred after 2 pm on 19 October. As the pyjamas were not sold to Crippen earlier than 1908 but the prosecution had already proved that the remains had been in the ground only about eight months, there was no need to call Chilvers to give evidence. That is, until Crippen stated that he had worn out and discarded the pyjamas in question years before the disappearance of his wife, at which point the judge had rightly allowed the prosecution to call evidence in rebuttal. This seems rather a disingenuous argument, as the statement about dates was elicited from Crippen on 21 October in reply to a direct question from Muir, who by then had Chilvers's evidence.

Curiously, Tobin made no reference to the fact that it might have been impossible for his client to receive a fair trial: the numerous reported confessions and the burial of the remains a week before the trial were almost certainly prejudicial, but neither Newton nor Crippen seems ever to have made an issue of this. Newton mentioned it briefly, but given his links with Horatio Bottomley MP, the proprietor of the weekly *John Bull* (who paid for the appeal and soon published yet another false confession), it might be argued that his loyalties lay elsewhere.

The appeal court judges made short shrift of Tobin's arguments, holding that the trial judge had clearly laid out the law regarding onus of proof, and had acted well within his discretion in admitting Chilvers's testimony. If Muir had set a trap for Crippen, that would constitute a miscarriage of justice, but there was no reason to suppose this had happened. So far as the remains' identity was concerned, the judges were unsurprised that the jury trusted the testimony of the prosecution experts over that given by the defence — cross-examination had revealed the obvious weaknesses in the opinions of their medical witnesses. The appeal failed, and the execution was rescheduled for 23 November. Dr Crippen had less than three weeks to live.

PUBLIC REACTION

Michael Gilbert notes in *Dr. Crippen* that even after the appeal was dismissed public excitement continued to grow rather than diminish. There is much evidence of that in the Home Office files (HO 144/1718/195492). Many people had doubts about the conviction, and argued that the body's identity and even its status as a murder victim were not clearly proved. James McGlashan, an elderly chemist, proposed the ingenious theory that the 'victim' had herself obtained the remains from a medical student (who made the bones into a skeleton), put hyoscine into them, buried them under the cellar floor and decamped with Bruce Miller (or someone else) to cause trouble. Alleged sightings of Belle Elmore in Liverpool, Dublin, Brussels and—in a widely circulated report—Alberta, and letters purporting to come from her, fed the media frenzy.

Many letters sought mercy for Crippen, and one threatened the Home Secretary, Churchill: 'You are a damn waster. How would you like to be hung for what you have not done? If Mr H.H. Crippen is hung on Wednesday you and the judge and jury will be in danger of your lives so take heed.' Only one writer, calling himself 'Nemesis', was adamant that a merciless killer like Crippen should be shown no mercy, while a woman who withheld her name entreated him to make his peace with God. Crippen saw none of these letters.

Prison officials also withheld dozens, perhaps hundreds of letters sent to Crippen by hoaxers and curiosity-seekers. There was a series of begging letters, mainly from Germany and Scandinavia, where the offer of 250,000 marks to Crippen by Professor Munyon was widely reported. The many bibles he was sent were not passed on due to sheer volume of numbers, but prison officials did allow him to see a telegram which came from Tennessee a week before the execution. It was either in code ('Hope Gewgaw, Smitchds') or a sick joke.

Dr Frank Clifford in Bournemouth came upon an old hypodermic case containing eight phials of hyoscine hydrobromide prescribed in doses of, he thought, one-tenth of a grain, proving that there was once a legitimate medical reason for giving such a large amount. Civil servants dismissed this as an error: 'The label on the bottle probably means that the contents equal one tenth grain, i.e. each [dose] equals one eightieth grain.'

There can be no doubt that there was public support for Crippen. On 7 November magistrates in Cambridge gently refused the offer to be hanged in his place made by an eccentric old soldier, while a petition organized by Arthur Newton gathered 15,000 signatures. When a reprieve was sought, the suggestion was made for the first time that it had been impossible for Crippen to have a fair trial: the newspaper coverage which alleged that he had actually confessed to murder (proved by the fact that several papers were fined for this libel) could have swayed the impartiality of any juror.

As the date of the execution drew nearer, complaints were made about the fact that, according to press reports, Crippen was permitted to see Ethel Le Neve under special circumstances that had not been granted to other prisoners recently executed. The Home Office looked into this, only to find that there had been no difference in treatment: condemned prisoners were allowed visits in a special room, sitting at each end of a long table with a prison officer on either side, and were always permitted a visit from their family on the day before execution. Ethel visited Pentonville as often as she was allowed, usually arriving after dark to avoid recognition; prison officials suggested that she should come in a cab, not a motor car, which was too open.

Among the most interesting of the letters that remain in the Home Office files are several which purport to come from Belle Elmore. The first arrived at Brixton prison in mid September, and although it was sent to the Secretary of State it has not survived. The next letter was redirected to Pentonville from Brixton. Written in Chicago on 22 October and posted two days later, this letter must initially have caused a few raised eyebrows:

> Doctor:
> As I saw your conviction coupled with the death penalty, I come from seclusion long enough to try and save your worthless life at least; as I don't want to be responsible for your demise, if I can save you in this way, but I will never come forward person- ally, as I am happy now. I informed the judge, now save yourself.
> Belle Elmore Crippen

Although suspicious of its origins, Home Office officials sent it to Scotland Yard to have the handwriting checked; two days later, and probably to everyone's great relief, they reported that the writing was not that of Mrs Crippen. Subsequent letters took a slightly different approach: although all claimed to be written by Belle, their common theme was one of a mysterious captivity which prevented her coming forward. As the date of the execution drew nearer, politicians and civil servants took the view that all such letters must be hoaxes and simply filed them away. The last arrived on the eve of the execution. Sent to the prison governor, Major O. Mytton Davies, it made a final plea for Crippen's life:

> Sir, I implore you to stay the execution of Dr Crippen. For the last 4 months I have been confined in a lonely house here, and jealously guarded night and day. I have been totally ignorant of the outside world, but have just learned my husband's fate. They have told me of the 'trial'. Oh, what a mockery! I am free tomorrow, and will come to London and startle the world.

The letter was postmarked in London, though the writer claimed to be in the north of England — presumably thinking it a more suitable location to be held prisoner. By now apparently used to such things, Davies sent the letter to the Home Office, but assumed that no action would be taken. He was correct: a senior official received it at 11 pm on 22 November and added it to the already voluminous case file the next day, noting it as another hoax. As Churchill had observed in a memo of 19 November, 'The petition and various letters add nothing to the case put forward by the defence and disproved before the jury and the Court of Appeal. Let the law take its course.'

LAST HOURS

At 9.15 pm on 19 November the prison governor informed Crippen that his petition had failed. He broke the news as gently as he could, but it came as a great shock to a man who had still dared to hope that he would be able to live out his dream of sharing a life with Ethel Le Neve.

On the following day his farewell message to the world appeared in *Lloyd's Weekly News*, and included his signature and a photo of Ethel Le Neve dressed in her boy's clothing. Although Home Office officials assumed that the words had been penned by a journalist, they were in fact Crippen's own, abstracted and amplified by Le Neve from letters he had written to her; her request that he should be allowed to correct the draft was refused. The message dwelled on the unfairness of his conviction and his love for Ethel, and expressed his thanks for the kindness of the prison governor. He was ready to bow to the inevitable, and wrote his last letter to her on 22 November.

In 1910, the 'Crippen year', 16 men were hanged in Britain by five Home Office-appointed executioners working in pairs. Crippen was the thirteenth, hanged at Pentonville by John Ellis (a Rochdale barber who had been a hangman since 1901) and his assistant William Willis (a Mancunian appointed in 1906). Ellis was a man with a profound sense of duty, well known for his fussiness and attention to detail: his primary goal in every execution was speed and efficiency, and he developed a number of innovations designed to minimize the prisoner's suffering. One such innovation arose when he hanged Dr Crippen.

The third week in November was a particularly busy time for Ellis and Willis, who hanged men on three successive days.

On the 22nd they executed wife-killer Henry Thompson, a middle-aged alcoholic who had been found asleep in bed beside his wife's strangled body and who displayed a remarkable sang-froid until the end. After hanging Crippen the next day they shook off a journalist, caught a train to Reading and prepared for the execution of William Broome, convicted of murdering an elderly widow in Slough—a young man whom Ellis thought should have had the benefit of the doubt and who proclaimed his innocence on the scaffold. Of the three, Crippen was the most enigmatic and caused the least trouble, but Ellis found the media interest unusually nerve-racking.

His memoirs, *Diary of a Hangman*, provide a detailed account of Crippen's last hours. Ellis and Willis caught a train from Liverpool to London, arriving at Pentonville at 4 pm on the day they hanged Thompson. When Ellis got his first look at Crippen he was impressed by his calm amiability, later recalling that 'I speak of men as I find them, and Crippen came across to me as a most pleasant fellow.'

Pleasant, yes, but he had a devious streak. On the night before his execution he made what appears to have been his only real attempt at suicide, a botched effort involving a fragment of broken glass from his spectacles that the warders who had been detailed to watch him quickly discovered. That was at midnight; the execution was scheduled for 9 am the following morning, 23 November 1910.

Ellis woke at 6.30 to check the scaffold and make his final

preparations. He had been told by the under-sheriff of London, Frederick Kynaston Metcalfe, that Crippen was about 5ft 4in tall and weighed 136 lb, and that a drop of 7ft 6in would therefore be appropriate. In fact Crippen had gained weight since his first admission to Brixton prison and was now 142 lb; when Ellis saw him he decided to add another three inches to the drop, a decision which caused an argument after the execution.

Crippen also woke early and dressed in his own clothes, the grey frock coat he had worn at Bow Street and a collarless shirt, before attending a special mass. Although he appeared entirely calm (the prison officers seemed more miserable than he did), he was unable to eat much of his breakfast. He spent the last hour of his life with Thomas Carey, the Roman Catholic prison chaplain, and two warders. At 9 am Ellis entered the condemned cell and pinioned Crippen, who submitted without a word and actually looked much brighter than most of those Ellis had seen in similar circumstances. The rest took place in the space of about one minute.

Ellis had already decided to adopt a new procedure suggested to him by the chief warder: instead of walking behind the prisoner to the gallows, he immediately left the cell and went to stand on the scaffold, so that he was there waiting when Crippen came in with Willis and the other officials who were to be present. This saved time and avoided last-minute confusion, so much so that he made it his usual practice in every execution afterwards, doubtless saving prisoners (and witnesses) from needless distress. Crippen displayed real bravery, and Ellis recalled that he was smiling as the white cap was placed over his head. And then the execution itself:

> In a trice he was on the trap-doors with his legs strapped together and a rope round his neck. One swift glance round to be assured that all was right, and my hand shot to the lever. Thud! the fatal doors fell. The slack rope tightened, and in an instant was still. Dr Crippen was dead.

As soon as Crippen had dropped, the prison doctor, J.H. Parker Wilson, checked his heart and signed the death certificate. The body was left hanging for an hour and then taken to the prison mortuary where first an autopsy and then an inquest were held. The form recording the details of the execution noted that his neck had been broken and there was 'no destruction of soft parts' (no blood was shed, happily for all concerned), but the doctor complained about the fact that every bone in the neck had been broken—the drop was too long. Ellis thought this rather a good thing, however, as death must have been instantaneous.

Ironically, the inquest was held before Walter Schröder, the same coroner who had insisted that the remains from the cellar be buried in Belle Elmore's name. He recorded the deceased's profession as 'dentist and doctor', a small courtesy Crippen would surely have appreciated.

An hour later, Dr Crippen was buried in the graveyard of Pentonville prison.

CHAPTER FIVE

The Mild-Mannered Murderer

According to legend, there were two rather romantic occurrences on the day of Crippen's execution. One myth holds that he was buried with Ethel Le Neve's photograph and letters, the other that she sailed for North America to begin a new life. Neither is true.

Prison records indicate that far from asking to be buried with a photograph of Ethel, Crippen actually asked for it to be returned to her with the rest of his belongings. She wrote to the prison governor on 24 November (PCOM 8/30) asking for his property (including the clothes in which he was executed, which were burnt some days after). Although the Prison Commissioners had no objection to returning the photograph, they referred the matter to the Home Secretary because Crippen had written an unauthorized farewell message on the back. It is not known what the message actually said.

Winston Churchill agreed in December that Le Neve could have the photograph, and her solicitors (she was no longer represented by Newton) advised in a letter of 21 December

1910 that anything for her should be sent to them, as she was 'away in the country' (PCOM 8/30). Probably the photograph and perhaps Crippen's letters too were forwarded to her at the end of the year, for they are not listed in the inventory made at Pentonville in August 1911 (PCOM 8/30; see plate 25), when she again applied for his property. This included his spectacles, six books, socks (no shoes, which must have been burnt), ten collars, four shirts, five handkerchiefs and just one pair of underwear.

Probate on Crippen's will was granted on 8 February 1911; he left assets valued at £268 6s 9d. Le Neve was his executrix, and promptly became embroiled in a civil action over his wife's estate. Because Belle died intestate her property (worth £175) should have passed to her husband, but her sister Theresa Hunn opposed this, with the support of the Music Hall Ladies Guild. The judge ruled in favour of Mrs Hunn, as neither convicted felons nor their representatives could profit from their crime (*The Times*, 7 and 14 February 1911). Ethel had argued that Crippen's conviction did not prove he was guilty of murder, which is perhaps indicative of a genuine and enduring belief in his innocence.

The man who made history by sending the wireless message that led to Crippen's capture, Captain Kendall of the *Montrose*, was paid the £250 reward, but instead of cashing the cheque, he framed it. The only other recorded claim to the reward came from two Canadian journalists who believed they had been the first to inform Scotland Yard of Crippen's flight to Canada.

Superintendent Froest dismissed this—they had not provided the crucial lead (MEPO 3/198).

Walter Dew, who seems to have had a soft spot for Crippen, retired on 5 December 1910 at the age of 47, after serving over 28 years with the Metropolitan Police. He profited richly from a number of libel suits against newspapers that had printed one lie too many during the case, and then became a private investigator. He died in 1947, still famous as the man who caught the most infamous murderer of the first half of the century.

In June 1911 Arthur Newton was found guilty of professional misconduct by the Law Society and suspended for 12 months: he had helped Horatio Bottomley create the entirely fictitious Crippen confession published in *John Bull* (HO 144/1719/195492). In 1913 he was convicted of fraud and jailed for three years. A decade later Bottomley too went to prison for fraud.

In November 1910 the police paid the rent on 39 Hilldrop Crescent to the end of the year, the landlord considering it a fair exchange for the damage caused during the investigation. A succession of tenants passed through the once most famous house in England until it was destroyed by a German bomb in September 1940.

And what became of Ethel Le Neve, the woman at the centre of the mystery? At the end of 1910 the governor of Pentonville thought she had left England, which suggests that such a rumour had begun to circulate, but she was evidently somewhere in the country. Where did Le Neve go after November 1910, if not to North America? In his recent book *Supper with the Crippens*, David James Smith traced her movements: she went to Canada briefly in 1912, then lived for three years as Ethel Harvey in Battersea from 1913 and married a clerk named Stanley Smith on 2 January 1915. She never revealed her identity to him or their two children, and lived out her life in Croydon, dying at Dulwich Hospital on 9 August 1967, aged 84. If she knew what happened at 39 Hilldrop Crescent in the early hours of 1 February 1910, she took the secret to her grave.

WHAT REALLY HAPPENED?

People have been speculating about what really happened to Belle Elmore ever since her remains were excavated from the cellar of her home. There is no doubt that they were her remains, or that she was killed and dismembered by her husband: no one has ever seriously suggested otherwise. In July 1910 police interviewed John McCrindle, a carter who claimed to have removed boxes from 39 Hilldrop Crescent for a woman resembling Belle, suggesting that she had indeed run off. The details of his story were inconsistent, however, and if it was true, the incident happened two weeks before she disappeared (MEPO 3/198).

As Michael Gilbert says: 'What is of interest is the continued and continuing curiosity about the Crippen case.' Everyone involved had a theory, and numerous others have been suggested over the years, but all share an essential similarity, focusing upon three key questions. Why did Crippen kill Belle, and why in January 1910? What happened to the rest of her body? And what did Ethel Le Neve know?

After Crippen was hanged, Muir is supposed to have commented, according to his biographer Sidney Felstead, that 'full justice has not yet been done'. This must be an oblique reference to Le Neve knowing that Belle was dead, not simply gone away. The fact that she never testified allowed her to avoid the difficult questions, such as whether she did indeed sleep at the house on 2 February. And David James Smith has pointed out that Le Neve announced her engagement to friends in January 1910, before Belle disappeared.

As to motive, Muir was right to suppose that Ethel lay at the heart of the matter. His assumption that Crippen suffered financial worries and that his life with Belle was one of unending misery is less persuasive, but all commentators agree that the marriage was not a happy one. Humphreys, for his part, 'never looked upon Crippen as a great criminal': in his view, Crippen committed a crime of passion, and Ethel Le Neve was so devoted to him that she never questioned his actions. As Stanley Jackson relates in *The Life and Cases of Mr Justice Humphreys*, F.E. Smith recalled Crippen as a 'brave man and a true lover'.

The earliest theories were suggested by Filson Young, the journalist who edited the trial transcript for publication. He dismissed the official prosecution line, that Crippen killed his wife so he could be with Le Neve, as insufficient: he could have left Belle at any time. Young was most persuaded by the theory that money lay at the heart of the matter: Belle threatened to leave, empty the bank account and take her property with her. In January 1910, Young alleged, she had told friends that this was her intention if Crippen did not end his affair; if she left, Crippen would not have had the means to look after Le Neve in the way he wished to do. A review published by the *Daily Mail* in February 1920 found this reasoning persuasive (HO 144/1719/ 195492), as did Bechhofer Roberts in his biography of Humphreys, but Gilbert and Smith do not: Crippen was perfectly capable of earning a good living, and the money was safe in the bank until December 1910. Why kill Belle in January?

A third theory (its origin is unknown but it has been attributed to Edward Marshall Hall, who was rumoured to have refused the brief because Crippen would not allow him to use this line of defence) holds that Crippen accidentally overdosed Belle with hyoscine, in an attempt to restrict her sexual demands on him or to knock her out so he could bring Ethel into the house—presumably for sex. If he had reported the death he might have made Ethel an accomplice, subject to the full glare of an inquest, if not a charge of manslaughter.

This theory fails on all counts: it is unlikely that Belle and Crippen were still having sex regularly; that Ethel would agree to have sex with him while his wife was in the house;

that he would choose hyoscine over morphine or cocaine to drug her; or that he could make such a serious dosing error. However, it is worth pointing out, as two MPs did in an article published in *Reynolds News* in 1948, that most poisoners know when their victim will die and are able to plan accordingly; Crippen in contrast seems to have been surprised by a death he did not intend (HO 144/ 1719/195492).

This raises a further possibility. Willcox thought a claim of accidental death would probably have succeeded if Crippen had called a doctor (and, according to his son, would have been content if it had been shown that Belle committed suicide), so why dispose of the body? Ingleby Oddie suggested that Crippen planned to poison his wife with hyoscine and pass her death off as natural, but was unprepared for its effects: she became delirious, he panicked and shot her, then had to destroy the evidence. Crippen had a gun, and some neighbours reported hearing screams and what sounded like a gunshot (MEPO 3/198). If he shot her, it must have been in the head: Pepper found no sign of trauma to the viscera.

In all probability fearing a libel suit, Young refused to discuss this theory, as it 'would involve the collusion of an accomplice'.

WHAT HAPPENED TO BELLE'S BODY?

No trace of Mrs Crippen's head or limbs was ever discovered, and although their fate was not integral to the drama that subsequently engulfed her husband, the passing of years has not lessened the public fascination with them. We may never know why or precisely how Crippen undertook the ghastly task of dismemberment, but we can make some educated guesses about how he disposed of the grisly remnants.

The police did attempt to trace the rest of Belle. On 31 August the drain connecting 38 and 39 Hilldrop Crescent to the main sewer was checked, but no human detritus was found. In September, left luggage at railway stations around London was inspected and some parcels opened, but no bones or even bad smells were located (MEPO 3/198). A limb found in the Thames at Greenwich (which Pepper examined) probably prompted Froest's suggestion that Theresa Hunn should be asked whether her sister had ever had a broken leg. Nothing came of it.

The local rubbish collector reported removing large amounts of burnt refuse, mainly women's clothing and paper, from 39 Hilldrop Crescent during February; there were no bones. In his autobiography Dew stated that there were two theories of how and where the other parts of the body were disposed of:

> One is that he burned them in the kitchen grate at 39 Hilldrop Crescent, though none of the neighbours to whom I spoke ever noticed the offensive smell one would have expected if such were the case. The other … is that Crippen threw the missing remains overboard from a cross-Channel steamer. On 23 March he took Miss Le Neve over to Dieppe for Easter.

Neither suggestion withstands close scrutiny. Ethel would presumably have noticed had her lover brought a head or other body parts on holiday with him (but perhaps she knew all along?), and Dew's point about the smell that burning would cause was valid. It is far more likely that, like many murderers before, Crippen simply disposed of his wife in the nearest body of water, probably Regent's Canal.

Edward Schafer, professor of physiology at Edinburgh University, wrote to Pepper with precisely this suggestion on 23 October 1910 (DPP 1/13). He asked whether the canal had been dragged 'for the remainder of Mrs Crippen', as it was the easiest way to dispose of the parts that would sink. He suggested that the skin and viscera were deliberately buried because Crippen thought they would be destroyed by lime, or just less likely to be found — this was important because they contained damning evidence of poison, and the identifying scar.

Many people have wondered why some parts of the body were buried in the house while the rest was successfully disposed of, and why Crippen used lime at all. Some, including the prosecution lawyers, assumed this was merely a blunder. According to Willcox in a 1924 lecture, Crippen had 'the little knowledge that is dangerous'. He knew that quicklime could decompose a buried body, but did not know its effects would be altered by damp surroundings: it turned to slaked lime, which by a series of chemical reactions then formed adipocere. Crippen, who was always cool under pressure, was not such a bungler that he would have used slaked lime instead of quick-lime, and Schafer's theory helps to explain why he kept such incriminating physical evidence.

It does not, however, explain why he left his pyjama jacket in the grave, when it could so easily have been burnt along with all the other bits of clothing (which were almost certainly used to transport body parts to the cellar from the kitchen, the most likely site of the dismemberment). Erik Larson implies that they were simply overlooked in the somewhat dark environment. Perhaps that was it; or maybe it was hubris, a rare break in concentration, or plain stupidity.

A PERSONAL VIEW

The public fascination with the story of the little American doctor has long fostered stereotypical images of the three principal characters in the tragedy: Crippen, the cold-blooded killer who deserves our sympathy; Belle, the unfaithful shrew; and Ethel, the weak-willed girl. Although the documents in the National Archives cannot reveal what these people really thought or knew, they do give us some additional insights into their activities and characters.

I agree with other writers on the case: Crippen was determined to protect Ethel at the cost of his own life. Everything that happened revolved around his love for her—what she wanted and what he would do to make her happy. She was, after all, the source of all his happiness.

There is no firm evidence that she knew he had killed his wife, but if she was in the house on 2 February, as Crippen said at his trial that she was, it is difficult to see how she could have avoided noticing that something was amiss. She herself placed the date a few days later: one of them was lying (or mistaken), but given Mrs Jackson's uncertainty about dates, it is impossible to say who. It is remotely believable that she was there on 2 February, saw nothing (if she did not go to the basement), and really believed in his innocence. However, on the whole it seems probable that she knew more than she was willing to divulge.

Why did Crippen kill Belle when he did? His lover was tired of being a mistress and wanted to be a wife. She must have made this clear to him more than once — perhaps through her disappearance to Brighton and dalliance with Stonehouse — and told Emily Jackson that Belle was on the verge of leaving, after which Crippen would divorce her and marry Ethel. If he led her to believe this and then Belle refused to go, that might have prompted the murder. Perhaps he was lying all along and Belle never threatened to leave. Similarly, this suggests that unless Belle did desert him, Crippen had no grounds on which to divorce her. The fact that they were Catholics may also have been relevant. As for the timing, that again probably had more to do with Ethel than with Belle: Crippen could not allow the love of his life to grow tired of waiting. The £600 was probably coincidental so far as the timing was concerned.

Why did Crippen flee after Dew's visit? If he had stayed, published the advertisement and brazened it out, he might have eluded his fate. Perhaps his iron nerve finally broke — John Nash's visit followed so quickly by one from the police must have been a rude shock to a man who had grown accustomed to his own lies. Why did Ethel go with him? That is more difficult to gauge, but her conversations with Emily Jackson and her behaviour after Crippen was sentenced to death give the definite impression that she was not prepared to abandon him.

Finally, it is clear that Crippen planned to kill his wife (her hair curlers, clothing and empty stomach imply that she died around breakfast time on 1 February), but the fact that he dismembered her suggests that something went wrong. On the other hand, that may have been the plan: he could have committed murder in a less messy way, but murder is never an uncomplicated business. At the end of the day, I take my cue from those who knew him: despite his many unpleasant qualities — liar, snake-oil salesman, adulterer — Crippen clearly had something that appealed to others, and this I think was for the most part his true character. He was calm, quiet, polite, kind, a good friend — not at heart a hardened killer. If he had not fallen in love with Ethel Le Neve, Belle Elmore would have lived out her natural days.

Ultimately, Dr Crippen appeals to our sense of romanticism: regardless of his cold-blooded deed, his love for one woman never wavered, and that speaks to the romantic within us all.

Sources & Reading

—

The original material cited here comes mainly from the Metropolitan Police, Home Office, Prison Commission, Central Criminal Court and Director of Public Prosecutions documents held by the National Archives. See the website www.nationalarchives.gov.uk.

The main files are: CRIM 1/117: depositions taken at the inquest and at Bow Street Police Court; DPP 1/13: records relating to the case for the prosecution, including copies of forensic reports; HO 144/1718/195492: Home Office correspondence on the police investigation and the trial, including a trial transcript and notes of the proceedings in the Court of Criminal Appeal; HO 144/1719/195492: Home Office correspondence on Crippen's imprisonment, appeal, execution and will; MEPO 3/198: records of the police investigation, including witness statements; PCOM 8/30: documents relating largely to Crippen's imprisonment and execution.

The main publications on various aspects of the case include:

N. Connell, *Walter Dew: The Man Who Caught Crippen* (Sutton, 2005)

T. Cullen, *Crippen: The Mild Murderer* (The Bodley Head, 1977)

W. Dew, *I Caught Crippen* (Blackie & Son, 1938)

J.E. Early, 'Technology, modernity, and "the Little Man": Crippen's capture by wireless', *Victorian Studies*, 39 (1996), pp. 309–37

M. Gilbert, *Dr. Crippen* (Odhams Press, 1953)

J. Goodman (ed.), *The Crippen File* (Allison & Busby, 1985)

E. Larson, *Thunderstruck* (Doubleday, 2006)

E. Le Neve, *Ethel Le Neve: Her Life Story* (John Long Ltd, 1910)

D.J. Smith, *Supper with the Crippens* (Orion Books, 2005)

F. Young (ed.), *The Trial of Hawley Harvey Crippen* (William Hodge & Co., 1920)

The following biographies include useful information:

D.G. Browne, *Sir Travers Humphreys: A Biography* (George G. Harrap, 1960)

D.G. Browne and E.V. Tullett, *Bernard Spilsbury: His Life and Cases* (George G. Harrap, 1951)

J. Ellis, *Diary of a Hangman* (True Crime Library, 1996)

C. Evans, *The Father of Forensics: The Groundbreaking Cases of Sir Bernard Spilsbury, and the Beginnings of Modern CSI* (Berkley Books, 2006)

S. Felstead, *Sir Richard Muir: A Memoir of a Public Prosecutor* (The Bodley Head, 1927)

T. Humphreys, *Criminal Days* (Hodder & Stoughton, 1946)

S. Jackson, *The Life and Cases of Mr Justice Humphreys* (Odhams Press, 1952)

L. Randall, *The Famous Cases of Sir Bernard Spilsbury* (Ivor Nicholson & Watson, 1936)

B. Roberts, *Sir Travers Humphreys: His Career and Cases* (The Bodley Head, 1936)

P.H.A. Willcox, *The Detective-Physician: The Life and Work of Sir William Willcox, 1870–1941* (William Heinemann, 1970)

PICTURE ACKNOWLEDGEMENTS

Pictures can be seen at the National Archives unless another source is given here. **17, 20** Hulton Archive/Getty Images **18** Bettmann/CORBIS **21** Mirrorpix

AUTHOR'S ACKNOWLEDGEMENTS

I would like to thank Sheila Knight and the helpful staff of the National Archives, as well as Damian Mitchell, Nina Staehle, Anne-Marie Kilday and Cliff Williamson for their assistance in researching this book.

Index